JULIE ANN GO[]

Our boys 1914–1918

Who were the fallen of one Oxfordshire valley?

AlleyCat Books

First published in 2018 by AlleyCat Books
© Julie Ann Godson
ISBN-13:978-1722055479
ISBN-10:1722055472

The author has asserted their moral right
under the Copyright, Designs and Patents Act, 1988,
to be identified as the author of this work.

All Rights reserved. No part of this publication may be reproduced, copied, stored in a retrieval system, or transmitted, in any form or by any means, without the prior written consent of the copyright holder, nor be otherwise circulated in any form of binding or cover other than that in which it is published and without a similar condition being imposed on the subsequent purchaser.

A CIP catalogue record for this title is available from the British Library.

Front cover: *The Plough Boy* by Henry Herbert La Thangue
Back cover: *Henry Allen in Cricketing Whites* by Henry Scott Tuke

'Their name liveth for evermore'
Ecclesiasticus, chapter 44, verse 14

Contents

Introduction 7
Bert Akers 9
Arthur James Allen 13
Frederick Allen 16
Henry John Barnett 19
William E Barnett 22
John Baston 25
James Batts 28
Harry Belcher 31
Walter William Belcher 34
George Bolton 38
Albert Bowsher 42
Arthur Bradbury 45
George Bradbury 49
Roland Bullock 51
George Burden 54
Vernon Clifton 57
William Clifton 60
Arthur Coles 63
Dan Coombs 67
George Eaton 70
William Esson 73
George Herbert Florey 77
Percy Franklin 80

Henry Arthur Green 84

James H Green 88

Thomas Hudson 91

E B Johnson 94

James T Johnson 97

Harry Kelly 101

George James Kensett 104

Archibald James Knipe 107

Henry Knipe 110

Frederick William Loft 113

Frederick Miles 117

Cyril F Peart 120

Herbert T R Pickford 123

Tom Shepherd 127

C J Siret 130

Harry Sirman 133

Albert E Smith 136

Harry Talbot 139

John James Tidmarsh 142

Edwin Trinder 145

Thomas Trinder 148

Walter Victor Trinder 151

G E Tuckey 154

Ernest Walker 157

Percy Walker 160

Victor Cecil Walker 163

Charles Weston 167

Introduction

FORTY-EIGHT NAMES are listed on the three war memorials in the Lower Windrush Valley villages of Northmoor, Standlake, and Stanton Harcourt in Oxfordshire. In accordance with the feeling prevailing at the time that all the sacrifices made were of equal value, the names were listed in strict alphabetical order (unless a name was added after the original inscribing), with a notable absence of ranks or titles. This book adheres to the alphabetical approach, but includes ranks and regiments as a matter of historical record.

The memorials do not constitute a list of every man that went to the war from the village concerned. Put together by public subscription after the end of hostilities, they are a record of those living in the village who wished to see a loved one commemorated locally. Just as not every man named was born in the Lower Windrush Valley, so some of those who were born here are commemorated elsewhere, according to where parents, wives or relatives were living at the time a particular memorial was commissioned.

The aim of this book is to provide a glimpse of the men's lives with their loved ones before the war. Sadly, some boys went off to the Front so soon after leaving school that there is really very little to go on. But even this allows an opportunity to contrast the quiet lives they expected to live in Oxfordshire with the dramatic circumstances they actually went into.

The research for this book was made possible by the generosity of Andrew and Julie Williams, and thanks go also to Jenny Beilby, Julie Hankey, and Judy Webb.

Julie Ann Godson
August 2018

Bert Akers
*202267 Private, 1st/4th Battalion,
Oxfordshire & Buckinghamshire Light Infantry*
Stanton Harcourt

SOME TIME BEFORE the spring of 1890, a blacksmith called George Hunt hailing from Powick in Worcestershire caught the eye of Emily Akers, daughter of the landlord at the Harcourt Arms in Standlake. The arrival of a baby boy after the customary interval confirmed the nature of the situation, and the baby boy was baptised Albert George on 7th December. Emily and George were not married until six days later – hence the use of the Akers surname for the boy rather than Hunt.

The Harcourt Arms: Bert Akers lived here with his grandfather Charles

Charles Akers may have taken young Bert to the Great Ram Fair in Oxford in 1899

Giving the new family shelter provided no problem; the couple moved in to the pub. A year later in December 1891 Bert's sister, Florence Emily, was born, and further babies kept arriving so the Hunts moved to a house of their own, possibly the cottage known as the Old Smithy at the top of Black Ditch. Bert was left in the care of his grandfather at the Harcourt Arms.

As well as being a publican, Emily's father Charles Akers was a comfortably-off farmer and miller. Charles Akers was proud of his hogs, entering them in the annual Christmas Meat Fair in Oxford. He probably took his eight year-old grandson Bert along when he set off to buy Oxford Downs sheep at the Great Ram Fair in Oxford in 1899.

Ten years after the hasty marriage of Bert Akers' parents, Emily's brother

The Old Smithy at the junction of the main road and Black Ditch

Three blacksmiths and one apprentice were working in Stanton Harcourt in 1891

Frederick Akers married in some style at the church in Standlake. One wonders what were Emily Hunt's feelings as she surveyed the arrangements which included 100 wedding presents, four bridesmaids, and an organist shipped in from Eynsham. By the time of Emily's death in 1910 she had children aged 19, 18, 16, 13, 10, 8, 6, and 4. It seems distinctly possible, therefore, that she died in childbirth. She was 40 years old.

Back in the Akers household in 1911 eldest son Bert, now aged 20, spent his time helping in the Harcourt Arms along with his sister Florence. Since Bert's uncle William, a corn merchant, remained unmarried at the age of 42, it may be that Bert was under consideration to inherit the Akers business concerns. Bert's uncle Frederick was running F Akers post office, bakery, and grocer's shop opposite the pub. His uncle George worked the farm. Charles Akers' brother, Henry Thomas, was a miller at Beard Mill, and living with him was another of Charles's brothers, Thomas, who worked on the farm.

Bert's grandfather Charles Akers died in August 1911 at the age of 76. Probate was granted to Charles's son William and his own brother the miller Henry Thomas Akers. Charles's effects were valued at £3,392 10s 10d.

All day on 13th August 1916, the 1st/4th Ox & Bucks endured intense shelling in the trenches on the Somme. Amongst a heavy death toll was Bert, but it wasn't until almost a year later that his family was told. The *Witney Gazette* of 4th August 1917 reported that Bert's relatives had 'been officially informed of his probable death in action at about the middle of August last' when he had been reported missing. A lack of letters home had probably alerted them already to the possibility that all was not well with Bert. He was 25.

Arthur James Allen
32519 Rifleman, 1st/5th Battalion,
South Lancashire Regiment
Stanton Harcourt

WHEREAS THE MAJORITY of the men in this book are farm workers of one sort or another, Arthur James Allen was one of those village lads who decided to step off the agricultural treadmill. His father Richard Allen was a farm labourer who had married Sarah Russell in June 1883. Sarah already had an illegitimate son, Harry, born in 1873. At their home in Sutton, Richard and Sarah went on to have three children of their own, Ellen, Walter, and Arthur, the youngest, born in 1890. Sarah died when little Arthur was 8.

In 1901 Arthur's sister Ellen, 17, was still at home in Sutton running the household for her father Richard and two brothers. There seems to have been insufficient money to keep Arthur's elder brother in school, so at 13 Walter was working as a teamster on a farm, managing horses for haulage. Arthur, 11, may have developed a facility with the animals, as many young working men would have done in all sorts of occupations at that time.

This contact with horses perhaps contributed to Arthur's decision to take up work as a cab driver in Oxford. Using horses to haul people in cabs was doubtless more lucrative than using them to pull farm carts but, unlike a family living in a tied cottage, a cab driver would have to find his own accommodation. In 1892 Arthur's step-brother Harry Russell had married in Headington to Daisy Hazard. Harry worked as a college servant, potentially a job for life with a pension at the end for those who rose high enough. At the age of 21,

Arthur was living with his step-brother Harry Russell and family who took in boarders at their large house in the Cowley Road, currently the premises of James C Penny, estate agent.

Before the advent of the Oxford Bus Company in 1913, the only form of public transport within the city was the horse-drawn tram and cab. The people of Oxford dreamed of motor-buses, but the corporation considered them dangerous and dirty, preferring the cleaner electric tram. The University, needless to say, wanted no change at all.

Sited just north of the Martyrs' Memorial in St Giles was a cab stand offering shelter to waiting cabmen. An underground men's convenience was built in 1895 and was doubtless much welcomed by the cab drivers. By 1889, the St Giles cab stand was listed as a telephone subscriber with the number Oxford 59, and presumably the telephone was inside this shelter.

Another shelter was opened in Broad Street in July 1885. According to the *Oxford Chronicle*: 'The building is a very comfortable place. It was built by Messrs Bart, Axtell & Co at a cost of about £120. Under the seats are lockers, in which, through the kindness of Miss Acland and friends [fundraisers for the shelter], a number of books have been placed, and there is also a substantial tea and dinner service.'

The St Giles cab stand, just north of the Martyrs' Memorial

The cab stand on Broad Street was mounted on wheels so that it could be moved about

Miss Acland's father Sir Henry Acland KCB, an eminent physician who lived in Broad Street, explained in his speech that: 'On the table [the drivers] would find some of the good things, and he hoped they would make use of them. There were also good books in the lockers – he did not mean only religious books, but there were some good books on every subject. Miss Acland had subscribed for a daily paper, and he hoped they would make better use of it than some people did. He hoped from it they would acquire moderate views, and that they would not be violent for or against any mere party, but be thoughtful citizens looking to the well-being and happiness of all.' Evidently extreme views amongst cab drivers is not a new phenomenon.

After the German Spring Offensive of 1918 died down, the Allied counter-offensive began. On 2nd October the Germans began a large-scale withdrawal, pursued by the British. On 22nd October the 1st/5th Battalion, South Lancashires attacked Barges Chateau and mill about a thousand yards in front of its position but, although it reached the objective, it could not hold it.

Arthur's battalion continued active patrolling and raids. He died on 29th October 1918 at the age of 28.

Frederick Allen

16502 Private, 5th Oxfordshire & Buckinghamshire Light Infantry

Stanton Harcourt

HOW EXTRAORDINARY to think that Frederick William Alder Allen, born in Black Ditch in 1891, would die twenty-five years later on one of the most momentous days of the First World War – the day modern tank warfare arrived.

Stanton Harcourt agricultural labourer George Allen married Sutton Courtenay sawyer's daughter Rosa Alder in 1886. Frederick was their first boy,

The Allen home at The Elms, now 1 Steadys Lane

though they already had two girls, Alice Emily born 1887, and Ethel May born 1889. The precious boy was named after both his grandfathers, Frederick Alder and William Allen. Sadly, the Allens' first-born child, Alice, died aged 9 in 1896.

By 1901 they had moved to the main village street, and George was working as a carter on a farm. Ethel and Frederick had now been joined by Alfred George, Leah, Victor John, and baby Percival Stanley. But later that year, little 5 year-old Leah also died. Many parents in the Lower Windrush Valley knew well the anguish of losing children without any help from the machinations of politicians.

Ten years later the family was in a cottage in The Elms known today as 1 Steadys Lane. Ethel was in service in Oxford as parlour maid to a Fellow of Magdalen College and his family at their fourteen-roomed Victorian villa in Crick Road. At home in The Elms were Frederick, working as a farm labourer, Victor, and Percival, and now also Ivy Rose, Bernard Leslie, and Violet Miriam. No sign of Alfred: an Alfred George Allen had died in hospital in Oxford in 1906 aged 12, but the census return of 1911 is quite clear that the Allens lost two children, not three, and they would know.

Fred enlisted with the Ox & Bucks Light Infantry and was posted to the 5th Battalion. His younger brother Victor also signed up with the Ox & Bucks. Victor's enlistment papers of January 1915 show him to be a farm labourer before the war. They also show that he was promptly discharged six months later when it was discovered that he had lied about his age. He had claimed to be 19 (the legal lower limit for armed service overseas at the time) when he was, in fact, only 16.

The Mark I tank was the world's first tracked and armed armoured vehicle to enter combat. The name 'tank' was initially a code-name to maintain secrecy and disguise its true purpose. It was developed in 1915 to break the stalemate of trench warfare. It could survive the machine gun and small-arms fire in no-man's land, travel over difficult terrain, crush barbed-wire, and cross trenches to assault fortified enemy positions with powerful armament.

The British Mark I tank: first deployed on the day Frederick Allen was killed

On 11th September 1916 the entire fleet of Mark I tanks – forty-nine of them – began to move slowly into position for the Battle of Flers-Courcelette. Seventeen were unable to make it as far as the front line. Of the twenty-two that did, a further seven failed to work at zero hour. In the end only fifteen of the forty-nine tanks rumbled into no-man's land for the start of the attack on 15th September. And that was the day that Frederick Allen was killed in action, aged 25.

Reporting after the event, official historian Wilfrid Miles stated that the Germans had been 'dealt a severe blow but the attack fell far short of the desired achievement'. In fact, they were at first terrified. The British advanced 2,300 metres but the Germans quickly recovered and the Fourth Army was unable to exploit the advance due to exhaustion and disorganisation. However, the battle was a moderately successful set-piece attack by 1916 standards.

Fred is commemorated at Thiepval Memorial in north-east France, together with 72,000 other British and South African soldiers who fought on the Somme but have no known grave.

Henry John Barnett
18343 Private, 2nd Battalion,
Princess Charlotte of Wales's (Royal Berkshire) Regiment
Stanton Harcourt

HENRY JOHN BARNETT'S father, Appleton-born shepherd George Barnett, brings to mind Gabriel Oak, jobbing shepherd in Thomas Hardy's novel *Far From the Madding Crowd*, looking for work at the annual hiring fair. (Or, if you prefer, Alan Bates playing the part in the 1967 film version).

The fairs at Abingdon, Wallingford, and Burford took place at Michaelmas. They served as both a labour exchange for farm-hands and domestic servants,

Employers and workers met at hiring fairs: Hardy's Gabriel Oak and Bathsheba Everdene

Burford hiring fair: held at Michaelmas

and as an excuse for general jollification. Those seeking new positions sported the emblem of their occupation – woven straw for a thatcher, a curl of wool and a crook for a shepherd, cow-hair for a cowman, whipcord for a carter. A girl looking for work as a domestic servant might carry a mop, hence the alternative name 'mop fair'.

In George Barnett's case the imperative to find new accommodation and higher wages appears to have been his burgeoning family. He married Appleton needlewoman Eliza Woodwards in late 1886, and the first of their twelve children, Frederick, appeared the following year. In 1888 came Gertrude, and in 1891 Emma. Whether or not the move to Tubney was prompted by a growing brood, it's just as well that George did find employment there, because he and Eliza soon produced three more children: Henry in 1893, William in 1897, and Agnes in 1900. But their family still was not complete.

Next they were off to Dry Sandford, where there appeared Arthur in 1901, Walter in 1903, Ernest in 1906, Elsie in 1908, and Amelia in 1910. The older children were by 1911 working. The two eldest boys were still at home, 24

Henry's sister Emma worked at Sheepstead House, Marcham

year-old Frederick working as an under-shepherd and 17 year-old Henry as an under-carter. The two eldest girls were in service, 22 year-old Gertrude with two elderly sisters in Abingdon, and Emma as a kitchen maid at Sheepstead Park in Marcham, home of the Morlands brewing family. Three years later she would marry Appleton farm labourer Stephen Collett.

The first two weeks of Anglo-French offensive operations in the Battle of the Somme are known as the Battle of Albert (1st–13th July 1916). The Allied preparatory artillery bombardment commenced on 24th June and the Anglo-French infantry attacked on 1st July on the south bank from Foucaucourt to the Somme and from the Somme north to Gommecourt. From the Albert–Bapaume road to Gommecourt the British attack was a disaster, and this is where most of the roughly 60,000 British casualties of the day were incurred, including almost 20,000 dead. Henry John Barnett was one of the dead, killed in action on 1st July 1916. He was 23.

As a result of the changes brought about in society by the First World War, the hiring-fair aspect of the mops faded and the jollification aspect increased. There was no surplus of labour because there were many fewer men. Also, people of working age could read and were therefore able to check the situations-vacant column in the newspapers, or resort to state-funded labour exchanges.

In the years after the war, Henry's parents George and Eliza were living in Sutton, hence the inclusion of Henry on the Stanton Harcourt memorial. George Barnett died in 1932 aged 69. Eliza died two years later, also 69. Henry's older brother Frederick died in 1954 aged 67.

William E Barnett
17328 Private, 1st Battalion,
Princess Charlotte of Wales's (Royal Berkshire Regiment)
Stanton Harcourt

WILLIAM E BARNETT was a younger brother of Henry John Barnett (see page 19). He was born in Tubney in 1897 and, at the time of the 1911 census, he was only 13 and still at school. Before the next census was taken, William was dead. The only details we will probably ever know about his life are those given in the war diary of his battalion on the day of his death.

From 9th April to 16th May 1917, British troops attacked German defences on the Western Front in what became known as the Battle of Arras. On 28th April 1917 the 1st Battalion, Royal Berkshires was involved in fierce fighting all day. According to the battalion war diary:

'*Rollincourt Trench 28th April 1917*

'3 pm: Orders were received to prepare for an attack on Oppy Wood and vicinity that night. The time for attack was eventually put forward to 4 am.

'9 pm: The Battalion – less D Company – moved forward by Companies and relieved units of 6th Battalion in the front line, which was the same as that held previous to the attack. Relief complete 1 am 29th April 1917.

'*Front line east of Bailleul 29th April 1917*

'4 am: Battalion – less D Company – with troops on either flank attacked and captured the Oppy Line… The troops on our right failed to get in and the right flank was consequently exposed. At about 5 am the enemy commenced to bomb the right flank and fighting continued until about 10 am when, owing

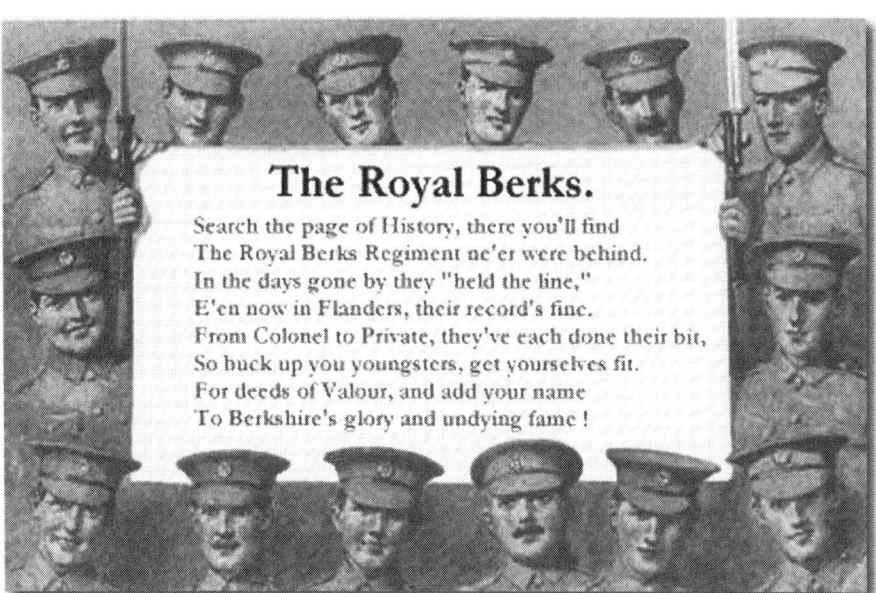

Oppy Wood, where William died, and (below) a recruiting postcard for his regiment

The Royal Berks.

Search the page of History, there you'll find
The Royal Berks Regiment ne'er were behind.
In the days gone by they "held the line,"
E'en now in Flanders, their record's fine.
From Colonel to Private, they've each done their bit,
So buck up you youngsters, get yourselves fit.
For deeds of Valour, and add your name
To Berkshire's glory and undying fame !

to lack of bombs and small arms ammunition, we were forced to give way, and withdrew to the jumping off trench via Sunken Road… C Company on the left withdrew northwards along the Oppy Line and placed themselves under the orders of the 17th Royal Fusiliers, establishing a block… taking with them three captured machine guns. The enemy shelled our front line heavily throughout the remainder of the day and there was a great deal of machine gun and rifle fire. Patrols were sent out at dusk and found the Oppy Line still held by the enemy.

'11 pm: The Battalion was relieved by the 13th E Yorks and returned to the trenches E of Rollincourt through a barrage of gas shells without sustaining any casualties.

'About 70 prisoners and three machine guns were captured by the Battalion during the day, and severe casualties were inflicted on the enemy.'

There then follows a list of seven officers killed, wounded, or missing. Of the other ranks, 15 were killed, 89 wounded, and 47 missing, making a total of 151 out of the 250 men originally committed to the attack. William E Barnett was among the 47 missing; his body was never found. He was 19.

The war diary concludes for the month of April 1917 with the laconic:
'Rollincourt Trench 30th April 1917
'Battalion rested during the day. Weather fine and warm.'

Almost 35,000 soldiers of the forces of the United Kingdom, South Africa and New Zealand who died in the Arras sector between the spring of 1916 and 7th August 1918 have, like William, no known grave.

Designed by Sir Edwin Lutyens, the Arras Memorial is located in the Faubourg d'Amiens British Cemetery, in the western part of the town of Arras. The memorial is inscribed with the names of all of those whose bodies were never found. The Stone of Remembrance by the memorial was also designed by Lutyens, and the inscription 'Their name liveth for evermore' is a bible quote selected by poet Rudyard Kipling, who lost his only son at the Battle of Loos in 1915. Similar stones can be seen at sites including a thousand graves or more.

John Baston
45803 Private, 5th Battalion,
Princess Charlotte of Wales's (Royal Berkshire) Regiment
Standlake

WHEN JOHN BASTON and Edith Annie Coombs celebrated their spring wedding at the Church of St Giles in Standlake in 1907 they had, like so many other young couples in those early years of the twentieth century, no idea how their fortunes would be dictated by international forces outside their control.

John was 26, having been born in Rack End, Standlake in December 1881;

Rack End, Standlake

The waggoner balances the load, while the young under-carter steadies the horses

Edith was five years younger. By the outbreak of war in August 1914, John and Edith had recently added baby Rona to their family of three other daughters, Dorothy May, 10, Elizabeth Ellen, 9, and Janet Lavinia, 7. John worked as a waggoner on a farm to support his wife and girls.

John signed up with Princess Charlotte of Wales's (Royal Berkshire) Regiment, and was deployed to the 5th (Service) Battalion. Formed at Reading on 25th August 1914, it moved initially to Shorncliffe and then on to Folkestone in January 1915. The battalion arrived at Malplaquet Barracks at Aldershot on 1st March 1915. On 31st May 1915 the men landed in France.

The 5th saw its first action in 1915 at Loos, then at the Battles of Albert, Pozières, and Le Transloy in 1916. During 1917 it took part in the First Battle of the Scarpe, the Battle of Arleux, the Third Battle of the Scarpe, and the Cambrai operations. John died nine days before the armistice on 2nd November 1918. The fact that he was buried at Hautmont Communal cemetery in northern France, close to the border with Belgium, suggests that he had been wounded and taken prisoner by the enemy.

Wounded prisoners benefited from the 1864 Geneva Convention, article 6 of which stated: 'Wounded or sick combatants, to whatever nation they may belong, shall be collected and cared for.' But care was rudimentary and amputation was commonplace, apparently even when unnecessary.

Some of the wounded, instead of being transported to the hospital, were despatched on the field of battle by German soldiers. One witness reported in 1918: 'Men wounded the day before were calling them from afar and asking to drink. The Germans finished them off by butting them with their rifles or bayoneting them, then despoiling them. I saw this from several metres away. A group of seven or eight men, felled by machine-gun crossfire, found itself at that point. Several were still alive, as they were begging the soldiers. They were finished off like I just said, shaken down and heaped up in a pile.' The Germans immediately denied this.

Hautmont was captured by the Germans in the early days of the war. The communal cemetery was used by the German troops for the burial of their dead, and the Allied prisoners who died in the local German hospitals were buried there by the town authorities. A war plot was formed outside the south-east part of the cemetery, which was later extended to enclose it. Six days after John Baston died, Hautmont was retaken by the 42nd (East Lancashire) Division on 8th November 1918. Three days after that, the fighting was over.

Edith Baston remarried two years later to Standlake farm labourer Frank Douglas. Edith and her new husband appear to have migrated to the Faringdon area, because three of Edith's daughters married there: Dorothy married John Cox in 1932, Elizabeth married William Kitchener in 1934, and Janet married Charles Curtis in 1936. Only youngest daughter Rona's marriage to Norman Moss in 1934 was registered in Oxford.

James Batts
*2119 Gunner, 'B' Battery, 79th Brigade,
Royal Garrison Artillery*
Stanton Harcourt

DEVILISHLY-HANDSOME James Batts started life in a conventional enough way for a boy from Black Ditch in Stanton Harcourt, but he was already a military man long before war broke out. And when we learn that James was already working on the land at the age of 11, we can understand why he felt the need to take his chances in the wider world.

James was born in 1879, the youngest of six children of cattleman Frederick Batts and his wife Ann Trinder. But in 1888, when James was 9 years old, his mother Ann died. This calamity explains why James was out at work two years later (and possibly before) – unusually early even for those days. The 1870 Elementary Education Act introduced compulsory education for children aged 5–13, but left the enforcement of attendance to school boards. Press reports show that parents were frequently summoned before the magistrates and fined for allowing their children to miss school; evidently Frederick Batts' predicament persuaded the school board to make an exception.

With an unpromising future to look forward to, James Batts struck out into the world and joined the army. At the age of 22, he was a gunner in the Royal Garrison Artillery billeted at Dover Castle. He completed his term of military service and returned to Oxfordshire, but not to Stanton Harcourt.

James took up work as a baker in Old Headington, lodging at Elmbank Cottages in Larkins Lane with an elderly couple. In October 1911 at St

James Batts: already a soldier before the war

Andrew's Church, Old Headington, James, now 32, married Elsie May Gammon. Ten years James's junior, Elsie was a local girl, the daughter of gardener John Thomas Gammon. James and Elsie lived in Old High Street, Headington, possibly at the New British Workman, the Temperance hostelry opened there in 1880. James continued to work as a baker, and he and Elsie had two children, James Frederick and Olive May.

Meanwhile James's old regiment the Royal Garrison developed from fortress-based artillery located purely on British coasts. From 1914 when the army possessed little heavy artillery, artillery grew into a major component of the British forces. The Royal Garrison was armed with heavy, large-calibre guns and howitzers that were positioned some way behind the front line and had immense destructive power.

James Batts was called up from the reserves and sent to France. He was wounded at the Battle of the Somme, and was presumably taken to hospital in Rouen, where he died of his wounds on 2nd September 1916 at the age of 38.

Royal Garrison Artillery training at the Citadel in Plymouth

Three months later his third child was born; Elsie named the little girl Joyce Nellie Somme Batts.

Elsie remarried from the New British Workman in 1923 (now 67 Old High Street, formerly number 27), suggesting that it may have been her marital home with James. Or perhaps her father had by 1923 become the caretaker. Elsie took James's three children and made a new life in her second husband's home city of Coventry. Her new husband was Henry Burden, a sewage works labourer.

James and Elsie's son James Frederick worked as a cinema manager and married Kathleen Weston in 1940. He died in 1980. Olive May is recorded as a charge-hand at an 'art silk works'; she married press tool maker William Manning in 1939. The silk works of Thomas Stevens & Co in Cox Street produced pictures woven in silk, including portraits of celebrities and local scenes, scriptural texts, hymns and psalms, and verses from the poets. Olive May died in 1985. Joyce was a clerk in the same silk works as Olive May; she married Walter Waddell, the family's lodger. Walter was a crankcase engineer, a crankcase being the housing for the crankshaft in an internal combustion engine. Joyce died in 2004.

The New British Workman in Headington

Harry Belcher
5825 Private, 1st Battalion,
Princess Charlotte of Wales's (Royal Berkshire) Regiment
Stanton Harcourt

HARRY BELCHER is a problem for the researcher. Although there was certainly a Belcher family in Stanton Harcourt at the time of the First World War, Harry's precise identity is unclear. There were two Henry Belchers in the village at the outbreak of the war, but they were aged 48 and 49, and therefore unlikely to have enlisted.

Village memorials took a while to organise, and often were not finalised until the early twenties. It may be that, by that time, the next-of-kin of another Harry Belcher had moved into the village and wished to have his name displayed there. Or perhaps Harry Belcher of the Royal Berkshires was simply a beloved relative of the Belcher family already resident in the village.

The regiment listed on the memorial also presents a problem. No Harry Belcher of the Welsh Fusiliers is currently evident in the record, but he may have enlisted with that regiment initially and later been transferred to another. It would be understandable if parents recalled – either with pride or anxiety – only the original regiment in which their sons enlisted.

The closest Harry Belcher geographically to Stanton Harcourt, and therefore the one most likely to be related to the family there of the same name, or whose relatives might have moved there after the war, is Harry Belcher of the Princess Charlotte of Wales's (Royal Berkshire) Regiment.

Harry was born in Goosey in 1880 to Alfred and Eliza, née Varney. In

BUSINESS AS USUAL!

The propaganda: reassuring images were sent home to relatives

1901 Alfred was a packer for the Great Western Railway, but by 1911 he was deemed disabled for work – perhaps no surprise when we learn that between them, Harry's parents had produced thirteen babies, though by 1911 only seven of those children were still living.

In 1901 Harry was absent from the family home, and the Welsh Fusiliers

The reality: the British released poison gas for the first time at Loos

were active in the Boer War at that time. His regimental number certainly suggests a pre-war enlistment, so he could have been called up from the reserves at the outbreak of the war to serve in the Royal Berkshires. But it would be rash to make any assertions based on such circumstantial evidence.

In his late twenties, Harry was working as a general labourer, perhaps alongside his younger brother Jim, who was a bricklayer's labourer. The family was now in Stanford in the Vale, so it was to Wantage that Harry travelled to enlist in the Ox & Bucks.

The British campaign in the spring of 1915 was referred to at the time as 'The Big Push'. The date 25th September 1915, the first day of the Battle of Loos, should be as notorious as 1st July 1916, the first day of the Battle of the Somme.

Over the previous four days, the German defences had been subjected to a continuous bombardment of 250,000 shells, but it had little real effect. Before sending in the infantry on the morning of 25th, the British released poison gas to make up for the ineffective artillery barrage. However a change in the direction of the wind at several points along the front blew the gas back into the British trenches, causing seven deaths and injuring 2,600 soldiers who had to be withdrawn from the front line.

In many places British artillery had failed to cut the German barbed wire in advance of the attack. German machine guns were particularly deadly for the British, killing 8,500 men in a single day – the greatest single loss of life recorded since the beginning of the war. Among them was Harry Belcher, killed in action at the age of 35.

Walter William Belcher
16634 Serjeant, 1st Battalion, Grenadier Guards
Stanton Harcourt

IT SEEMS UNLIKELY that the patrons of the hotel in genteel St Leonards on Sea upon whom young Walter William Belcher attended at Easter 1911 guessed that the 15 year-old lad serving them was capable of supreme courage. So many unexpected heroes were revealed by the First World War. In its absence these men might perhaps have gone through their whole lives without being obliged to extend themselves to the superhuman level that many did on the field of battle.

Eversfield Place in St Leonards on Sea near Hastings

Walter was born in East Challow near Wantage, the son of Henry, a cowman, and his wife Emma. Before the war broke out, Walter worked as a hotel waiter and lived in a boarding house in Eversfield Place in the popular seaside resort of St Leonards near Hastings. How could such a placement come about? It could be that during term times Walter was a college servant at the University.

Senior college servants like the steward of the dining hall, the butler, the head chef, or the porter, enjoyed advantageous working conditions and sometimes even a pension. But junior servants like the 'bed-makers' were employed on a casual basis, and laid off during the long vacations. Such an abrupt interruption to the household income of a poor family could be seriously problematic.

According to the *Victoria County History*: 'In 1860 the vice chancellor and mayor [of Oxford] set up a scheme to find employment for junior college servants during the long vacation in spas and seaside resorts, a practice which continued into the twentieth century.' The 1911 census, when we find Walter in St Leonards on Sea, was taken on 2nd April and not in the long vacation. But 2nd April was within the Easter vacation, so perhaps Walter did benefit from the scheme through a contact made in the previous summer. In 1916 he married Elizabeth Walker and the couple set up home in Sutton.

Walter joined the 1st Battalion, Grenadier Guards who found themselves at the end of the war fighting around Arras in northern France. He was promoted serjeant and on 23rd August 1918 the battalion was ordered to move east of Moyenneville in conjunction with the 2nd Division and capture Mory Switch trench.

On the morning of 25th the ground was covered in thick mist and the tanks which accompanied them could not find their route. Number 3 Company was unsupported when the tank they were following broke down. Their officer was wounded and they were down to 40 men so the officer ordered them to fall back. Other tanks were disabled because the Germans now had armour-piercing bullets. Heavy fire from the enemy forced the battalion to retire and they were driven out of Mory Switch by machine-gun fire.

However, the 62nd Division managed to deal with a counter-attack and this

THE GRENADIER GUARDS.
Facing the Foe.

allowed the battalion to retake Mory. It was now the turn of the 62nd to pull back but the 1st Battalion were able to maintain their position and clear Hally Copse of the troublesome machine-guns. They began the three-day operation with 489 men and 18 officers and ended it with 231 men and five officers.

For conspicuous gallantry in the face of the enemy, Walter William Belcher won the Distinguished Conduct Medal, regarded as second only in prestige to the Victoria Cross. According to *Visiting the Fallen: Arras South* by Peter Hughes: 'Serjeant Walter William Belcher DCM… won his award… after the enemy had made a determined attack in great strength and had penetrated a small section of the front line. He immediately organised bombing parties and led them with splendid courage and determination, driving back the enemy. The rapidity with which the enemy was ejected and with heavy losses was largely due to his excellent leadership and the example he set to his men.' He died on Sunday 25th August 1918. He was 24.

Elizabeth remarried in 1922 to Charles Mutton.

August 1918: Grenadier Guards after the battle in which Walter Belcher was killed

George Bolton
Leading Stoker, HMS Indomitable
Standlake

GEORGE CHARLES BOLTON was one of the most widely travelled of all our local servicemen. Born on 3rd February 1878, he was a ploughboy from Rack End in Standlake who went away to sea aged 21. His father Charles was a farm-hand and general labourer who had married Rosa King in March 1877.

Rosa died when George was 20, and this seems to have been the point at which George decided that he wanted more than a life of endless farm labour in the Lower Windrush Valley. Or was it that his parents would not give him permission to go and he had to wait until he came of age? The following summer he enlisted at the shore establishment HMS *Pembroke II* at Eastchurch near Sheppey in Kent, a Naval training school. His rank was stoker, second class.

Stokers did more than just shovel coal; they became experienced mechanics managing complicated boiler systems which regulated the speed of a ship according to orders coming down from the bridge. During his initial period of twelve years' service, George rose to stoker, first class. He served on a variety of ships and saw far-flung parts of the world under British influence.

On his return from his first ship HMS *Cossack* in 1903, George married Sarah Pratley of Langley near Shipton under Wychwood. Before her marriage, Sarah was in service in the Marriott household in High Street, Witney. The Marriotts had business interests in the coal trade, blanket manufacture and farming. Marriott, of course, is a name familiar to frequenters of the modern Marriotts Walk shopping centre to the west of the High Street.

The work of a stoker was tough and dirty, but he could become a skilled mechanic

During his years at sea before the war, George served on a variety of craft from battleships to torpedo cruisers, and visited destinations as widely spread as Canada, Bermuda, Sri Lanka and China. He spent two years on HMS *Woodcock*, a river gunboat patrolling the Yangtze river.

HMS **Woodcock**

The Yangtze river in China: George became more familiar with it than most of us will

Having completed his twelve-year engagement in 1911, George was transferred to the Royal Fleet Reserve, a reserve body of ratings and petty officers of the Royal Navy obliged to submit to a week's training at sea every year. Many hundreds of stokers were recalled to service from the Royal Fleet Reserve to form the naval battalions of the Royal Naval Division in August 1914. George joined HMS *Indomitable*, the world's first battlecruiser.

Indomitable was at the centre of some of World War I's most famous actions. In 1914 she was in the Dardanelles off Gallipoli, then in January 1915 at the Battle of Dogger Bank – where Admiral Beatty ordered his battlecruisers to make all practicable speed to catch the Germans before they could escape. *Indomitable* managed to exceed 26 knots (48 km/h; 30 mph) and Beatty recognised her performance, for which surely we must be allowed to give partial credit to Stoker Bolton, with a signal at 08.55: 'Well done, *Indomitable*.'

Having received treatment for 'muscular rheumatism', George returned to duty, now as leading stoker, just in time for the Battle of Jutland in May 1916. He returned to the Dardanelles in HMS *Theseus* later that year, and ended his career on the flagship *Europa* off Malta.

George was invalided out in July 1918 due to an aortic aneurysm, probably as a result of years of breathing in coal dust and very likely smoking too, like most sailors. His death was registered in Chipping Norton in 1919, twenty years after he originally enlisted in the Navy. George was 40 years old.

Recruitment poster

Albert Bowsher
59502 Private, 2nd Battalion, Worcestershire Regiment
Northmoor

THE BOWSHER FAMILY of the Lower Windrush Valley endured a constant struggle to make ends meet on meagre agricultural labouring wages. Every few years they were obliged to move around between Northmoor, Standlake, and Brighthampton, presumably following work and a home.

In the days when spelling was still somewhat fluid, Albert Bowsher was baptised Albert 'Bouchier' at the Church of St Denys, Northmoor on 1st September 1889. His father was Abraham, a shepherd from Childrey, and his mother was Northmoor-girl Matilda Webb, known by the family as 'Martha'. All three Bowsher sons, Henry George, Albert, and Solomon, were born in Northmoor.

In 1901 the family was living in Rack End, Standlake, where Albert's older brother Henry had already started work as an agricultural labourer at the age of 14. Then the family moved to Brighthampton where youngest brother Solomon worked with horses. Albert's occupation at the time is unknown; he was not at home on the day of the 1911 census. At the age of 22, he may have moved out, enlisted, or he might just have been away.

Two years later, Albert's mother Martha died at the age of 55. In the following June of 1914, 25 year-old Albert married Elizabeth Martha Brooks, a laundress from nearby Aston. Albert gave his occupation at the time of his marriage as 'shepherd'.

Late in the war Albert's regiment was ordered to attack the village of

Englefontaine on the Western Front. At 1.00 am on 26th October 1918 the new attack was launched. The enemy were strongly posted on the outskirts of the ruined village with machine-guns skilfully disposed to sweep the open ground. German machine-gunners opened fire as soon as the advancing platoons appeared out of the darkness.

In displays of astonishing individual bravery two machine-gun posts were captured; nevertheless there were many casualties. The attackers fought their way into the wrecked village and for a time a wild struggle raged around the ruins of the houses. Before dawn the German resistance was broken; and at first light on 26th October the last enemy troops in the village gave themselves up. Five men were killed and 34 wounded, among them perhaps Albert Bowsher.

Albert died a week after Armistice Day on 18th November 1918 of wounds received on the Western Front. He was 29. He was buried in St Sever Cemetery Extension near Rouen. This was close to several hospitals which included eight general, five stationary, one British Red Cross and one labour hospital, and Number 2 Convalescent Depot. A number of the dead from these hospitals were buried in other cemeteries, but the great majority were taken to the city cemetery of St Sever. In September 1916, the sheer number of bodies made it necessary to begin an extension, and this was where Albert was buried.

Northmoor: as a shepherd, Albert Bowsher would have moved wherever his work took him

The British Red Cross hospital at Rouen: before splinting came into use, a broken bone could lead to a soldier's death if an artery was severed during transportation

Albert's brother Henry ('Harry') joined the 5th Ox & Bucks and was killed in action during an attack on Bellewaarde Farm on 25th September 1915 (see page 45). The 5th Battalion's losses were 13 officers (out of 15) and 463 other ranks (out of 767). Harry is not listed on the Northmoor memorial.

After Albert's death, Elizabeth moved to Batchmore in Cleobury North near Bridgnorth. Albert's father Abraham Bowsher lived on for another twenty years after Albert's death and six years after Solomon's, dying aged 86 in 1938.

Arthur Bradbury
18072 Private, 5th Battalion,
Oxfordshire & Buckinghamshire Light Infantry
Stanton Harcourt

ARTHUR BRADBURY'S parents William and Honor came to Black Ditch in Stanton Harcourt for their retirement. William was a house painter from Twickenham and was aged only 33 when he described himself on the 1891 census return as 'living on own means', suggesting that he was in ill health. However, the country air of Stanton Harcourt appears to have revived William sufficiently for him to father five more children to add to 4 year-old John whom the couple had brought with them from Twickenham.

Let us hope that Honor enjoyed robust health because, when William died in December 1906 – in Headington which means that he was probably in hospital – she was left alone with five children at home aged between 17 and 9. Her big son, John, came to Stanton Harcourt to help his mother. At 24 in 1911 he was working as a coal porter. Joseph, 22, was boarding with a widow and her son in Ashford, Middlesex, and working as a grocer's carman (delivery driver). Percy was an agricultural labourer, and George was in service in Oxford as a page at the Broad Street rooms of Nevill Forbes, Reader in Russian at the University. Daughter Honor went into service back in Twickenham with three spinster sisters. With all these children earning, there seems to have been enough money to keep the youngest boys, Arthur and Frank, in school.

The Second Battle of Bellewaarde Farm on 25th September 1915 was an expensive diversionary attack launched to distract German attention from

Hurrah for the Oxford & Bucks. L.I.!

the Battle of Loos on the same day. Along with other regiments, the 5th Ox & Bucks were in the thick of it, and suffered heavily. During a preliminary bombardment at 3.50 am, the troops moved from their assembly trenches and at 4.19 am a mine was exploded as a signal for the attack to start.

A letter sent by a Lieutenant R Holloway of 9th Battalion, King's Royal Rifle Corps paints a harrowing picture of what the soldiers went through: 'At 4.19 am a mine that we had built under a German redoubt fifty yards from our trenches exploded; the mine was the signal for the 9th Rifle Brigade to advance. They found the German front-line abandoned except for look-out men and advanced to the second line which was lightly held. They carried it and prepared it for defence and advanced on the German third line. Meanwhile, we were waiting under heavy shell fire for orders to advance and support.'

At this point Lieutenant Holloway took a patrol out to see what was happening in the right: 'On my way back to report, I met two of our companies already advancing to support the 9th Rifle Brigade who were being bombed out of the German second-line trenches. The Rifle Brigade had lost all their officers and there was no organisation of their defences. After reporting the result of my patrol, I went up to join the Company again and naturally went to the [mine] crater. It was then about 7.45 am.

'The first thing I met was a messenger who shouted: "Our shells are dropping short, right in the crater!" The crater, when I got there, was an awful sight. There were more dead and wounded than living men. Almost as soon as I got in, one of our own shells burst right in the centre of the crater, blowing several men to bits, a sickening sight. I gave the order to evacuate; before I left, two more shells burst in the same place. As each cloud of earth lifted, one saw men who had been sitting there alive just before, toppled over with shattered skulls and limbs, and blood pouring from them.'

Arthur Bradbury was presumed dead on 25th September 1915. He was 18. The casualties sustained at Loos and the accompanying diversionary attacks made this the costliest day of the war so far. But Honor Bradbury's agony was not finished yet.

George Bradbury

200748 Private, 1st/4th Battalion,
Royal Hampshire Regiment
Stanton Harcourt

THE CONTRAST BETWEEN George Bradbury's life as a page in Oxford and his death in Mesopotamia could hardly be starker. As servants in the household of young, unmarried Oxford don Nevill Forbes, George and the cook Doris Strickland would frequently have had Forbes's apartments at 44 Broad Street, now the site of the new Weston Library, to themselves during vacations.

Life amid the dreaming spires of Oxford was hardly a preparation for the arid and dusty place George was sent to fight. Today we may, regrettably,

George Bradbury was in service in Broad Street, opposite the Clarendon Building

be familiar with images of Iraq, as it is now known; early twentieth-century Oxfordshire lads – not so much.

George appears, like his brother Arthur, to have signed up initially with the local regiment, the Ox & Bucks Light Infantry. But either heavy losses in the field or perhaps strategic concerns meant that men were frequently transferred between regiments. George found himself in the 1st/4th Battalion, Royal Hampshire Regiment.

The campaign in Mesopotamia was fought primarily between the British and Ottoman Empires in late 1915 and 1916. After the Ottoman Empire's entry into the First World War, Britain dispatched British and Indian troops to seize control of the Shatt-al-Arab waterway and the port of Basra in order to safeguard British oil interests in the Persian Gulf. Eventually, the Anglo-Indian force's mission evolved into the capture of Baghdad.

The British had been halted at Kut-al-Amara on 19th November 1915, and so the troops reinforced the position in order to face the Turks. The pursuing Turkish forces then surrounded the defenders at Kut in an attempt to cut them off from reinforcements and resupply. The siege of Kut was underway.

A detachment of the 1st/4th Hampshires was left to assist in the defence of Kut. The Turkish attacks culminated on Christmas Day when the defenders, including the Hampshires, were able to repel the Turkish onslaught. The Turkish commanders abandoned plans for an assault and chose instead to starve out the defenders.

On 21st January 1916 the rest of the 1st/4th were involved in a disastrous attempt to relieve Kut, losing 13 out of 16 officers and 230 out of 339 other ranks, including George Bradbury. He was 19.

British leaders then attempted to buy their troops out. A team of officers including T E Lawrence ('of Arabia') was sent to negotiate a secret deal with the Ottomans. In exchange for the release of the troops the British offered £2 million, equivalent to £150 million today, and promised they would not fight the Ottomans again. The Ottoman leader Enver Pasha ordered that this offer be rejected. Despite many further attempts to relieve the garrison the British commander in Mesopotamia, General Townshend, arranged a ceasefire on the 26th and, after failed negotiations, he simply surrendered on 29th April 1916 after a siege of 147 days.

By this stage the beleaguered defenders were in a terrible state, undernourished, exhausted, and riddled with disease. These men then went on to endure more than two years of Turkish captivity, an ordeal that only a few would survive.

Honor Bradbury moved back to Twickenham and made her home in Fifth Cross Road. She died aged 75 in Winchester in 1935. Arthur's sister Honor died unmarried aged 40 in Orsett in Essex in 1931. Frank died aged 82 in Abingdon in 1984.

The British base at Kut-al-Amara

Roland Bullock
8959 Private, 2nd Battalion,
Princess Charlotte of Wales's (Royal Berkshire) Regiment
Stanton Harcourt

UNLIKE MOST OF the men in this book, Roland Bullock was an out-and-out townie. He was born in Aston Street in Cowley in December 1886, and his father George Bullock was a plasterer. But his mother, dressmaker Maud Elizabeth Hudson, was a Stanton Harcourt girl.

George and Maud already had one son, Arthur George, by the time Roland came along. Roland was ten years younger than Arthur, and when Roland was only 4, Arthur had already started work as a printer's clerk. However, eventually Arthur followed his father into the plastering trade. In 1901 Arthur married Edith Emily Sansom, daughter of another plasterer from Mount Street, and the couple lived in Howard Street. Ten years later they had three children: Edna Dolores, 7, Archibald George, 6, and Gladys Muriel, 4.

Roland's parents separated, and in 1911 his mother Maud was back in Stanton Harcourt, living alone and surviving on her own means. His father George had moved to Lambeth and was still working as a plasterer at 55. Living with him in Stamford Street was widow Sarah Merryweather aged 48 whom George described in the census as his housekeeper. Sarah's two children, Edith, 26, and George, 23, were also in the household, listed as boarders. They were in fact the children of Sarah's marriage to William Merryweather, a railway guard.

By 1911, 24 year-old Roland was already Private Bullock of the 1st

Western Heights barracks at Dover Castle

Battalion, Royal Berkshire Regiment, living unmarried in the South Front barracks at Dover Castle on the Western Heights. He was later transferred to the 2nd Battalion.

From 10th–13th March 1915 Roland's battalion fought in the Battle of Neuve Chapelle. It was a British offensive intended to cause a rupture in the German lines, which would then be exploited with a rush to the Aubers Ridge and possibly Lille. According to *longlongtrail.co.uk*: 'Neuve Chapelle was the first large-scale organised attack undertaken by the British Army during the war. It followed the miserable winter operations of 1914–15… The battle opened with a 35-minute bombardment of the front line, then 30 minutes on the village and reserve positions. The bombardment, for weight of shell fired per yard of enemy front, was the heaviest that would be fired until 1917.'

A captain in the Ghurka Rifles later wrote: 'At 7.30 am the artillery bombardment commenced, and never since history has there been such a one.

You couldn't hear yourself speak for the noise. It was a continual rattle and roar. We lay very low in our trenches, as several of our guns were firing short.'

And *longlongtrail.co.uk* explains: 'Three infantry brigades were ordered to advance quickly as soon as the barrage lifted from the front line at 8.05 am. The Gharwal Brigade of the Indian Corps advanced successfully, with the exception of the 1st/39th Gharwal Rifles on the extreme right that went astray and plunged into defences untouched by the bombardment, suffering large losses. The 25th and 23rd Brigades of the 8th Division made good progress against the village. There were delays in sending further orders and reinforcements forward, but by nightfall the village had been captured… During the night the Germans reinforced their second line in front of the Bois de Biez, and all further attempts over the next few days brought little material success…

'The British losses in the four attacking divisions were 544 officers and 11,108 other ranks killed, wounded and missing. German losses are estimated at a similar figure of 12,000, which included 1,687 prisoners.' Roland Bullock died of his wounds on 11th March, aged 28.

George Bullock died in Lambeth in 1929 aged 74. Sarah Merryweather died in 1937 aged 75. Maud outlived them both, dying in Oxford in 1943 aged 90.

The village of Neuve Chapelle after the battle

Gilbert H Burden

*200627 Serjeant, 1st/4th Battalion,
Oxfordshire & Buckinghamshire Light Infantry*
Stanton Harcourt

TWO GENERATIONS of illegitimacy provide quite sufficient red herrings in the record to baffle any modern researcher into the origins of Gilbert Humphries Burden. But once the fog clears, the aim of the indviduals concerned appears to have been not so much to deceive as simply to fit in with society's norms.

Gilbert Robert Burden was born in Islip on 22nd June 1894 and baptised a full four months later on 22nd October. His mother is given in the parish record as 'Florence Burden', his father is unnamed (but perhaps that 'Robert', later dropped, is a clue). Florence would have been 16 when she gave birth to Gilbert, possibly only 15 when she conceived. In fact, Florence herself was the illegitimate daughter of Alfred Burden of Stanton Harcourt. Alfred had previously abandoned a wife and daughter in Eynsham where he worked as a 'gas maker' – a man who burned coal to produce gas for fuel. He appears to have fled south because he took up with Celia Humphries, a laundress from London who had also been married. In 1876, the couple had a daughter in Dover – Florence Humphries, Gilbert's mother.

Alfred and Celia returned to Oxfordshire, where Alfred set himself up as a poulterer in Mill Street, Islip. Celia and Florence adopted the name 'Burden', though it seems unlikely, if any attempt at deception was intended, that 'Humphries' would later have been used as Gilbert's middle name on his military papers. The name Burden was merely a signifier of where the two ladies slotted in to village life.

When Florence married widower Charles Nash in 1907, she gave her maiden name as 'Humpreys'. She and her husband, a tailor, lived briefly in Marlborough Road, Grandpont, then moved to Howard Street in Oxford, while 13 year-old Gilbert remained with his grandparents. The errant Alfred died in 1909 and his abandoned wife died in the same year, perhaps significantly in the Cowley workhouse, and describing herself as a 'widow'.

Also in 1909 Florence had a son named Charles Alfred, and then a second, Edward, in 1915. After Gilbert abandoned his work as a gardener to join up, his widowed grandmother Celia went to live in Sutton with relatives of Alfred's, Ernest and Florence Hudson, née Burden.

The Battle of Langemarck (16th–18th August 1917) was the second Anglo-French general attack of the Third Battle of Ypres. An unusually large amount

Mill Street in Islip

of rain in August, poor drainage and a lack of evaporation turned the ground into a morass, which was worse for the British and French who occupied lower-lying ground and were attacking areas which had been bombarded frequently and severely already. Mud and flooded shell-holes severely reduced the mobility of the infantry, and poor visibility hampered artillery observers and artillery-observation aircraft.

Gilbert Humphries Burden was killed in this hellish environment on the first day of the battle, 16th August 1917. He was 22. He left his effects to be divided between his mother Florence and his grandmother Celia.

Florence Nash died in 1936 aged 59. Her mother Celia Burden died in 1942 aged 93, and is buried in Stanton Harcourt. Desperately, one searches for some crumb of comfort in these tragic histories, and at least the Burdens did look after their own. A Burden descendant relates that Celia, who might so easily have been allotted the role of 'wicked lady', was in fact 'a much loved lady of all our family until her death, always dressed in black and looking very much like Queen Victoria'. One can only hope that Gilbert, who had lived all his life with Celia, knew that she would be cared for.

Langemarck, where Gilbert Burden met his death

Vernon Clifton

12033 Private, 7th Battalion, South Staffordshire Regiment
Northmoor

VERNON ALFRED CLIFTON'S mother, shepherd's daughter Fanny Bullock from Garford near Abingdon, had enjoyed mixed fortunes since her marriage to farm labourer Isaac Clifton, in 1878. She had given birth to eight healthy children, all of whom survived infancy. But her husband Isaac died aged 41 in 1896, leaving Fanny with a considerable challenge on her hands.

She took work as a charwoman and James and Sidney, her two eldest sons still at home at Clark's Cottage in Northmoor, helped support their four younger siblings. James worked as a farm labourer and Sidney as a ploughboy.

There was a clear distinction between a ploughboy and a ploughman. You had to be pretty brawny to steer a plough – not to mention experienced. The ploughman shouted directions at the boy, and the boy steered the horses accordingly. The horses followed the boy because he had care of them back at the yard – he fed and watered them. In this way, the boy learned the skills to take charge of the plough himself once he was physically strong enough. Sidney Clifton was only 14 in 1901 and, thanks to the meagre diet of the rural poor at the time, would have been small by modern standards.

Even with two boys working, it can't have helped when, in late 1908, Fanny was presented with another mouth to feed in the form of an illegitimate grandson. We can only assume that the family of the baby's unidentified mother was in an even worse financial position than the Cliftons.

The child's name (Vernon Alfred), coupled with the fact that Vernon Alfred

Vernon was banished to labour in the hamlet of Bayworth near Sunningwell

senior was all of 17 and unmarried when the child was born, strongly suggests that Fanny's youngest son Vernon was the father. Evidently it was deemed desirable to remove the disgraced Vernon from the village. He found work as an agricultural labourer in the hamlet of Bayworth near Sunningwell where he boarded with the Trinder family.

At the end of June 1915, Vernon Clifton sailed for Gallipoli with the 7th Battalion, South Staffordshire Regiment, landing at Cape Helles and remaining there from 23rd to 28th July 1915. The first casualties were sustained in the 'Horseshoe' facing Achi Baba – the main position of the Ottoman Turkish defences – but Vernon was not among them.

Following the failure to take Achi Baba, the battalion was then withdrawn to Imbros and rejoined the rest of division, landing at Suvla Bay near Lala Baba on 7th August. The landing was not a success and the troops were trapped on or close to the beaches. On the evening of the 8th August, the 7th Battalion received orders to push forward the following morning.

The advance started at about 5.00 am and proceeded in a satisfactory

Following the landings of August 1915, troops became trapped on the beaches of Suvla Bay

manner till 6.30 am, when the Turkish forces counter-attacked. A very heavy enfilade from enemy machine guns divided the British into isolated groups with no support coming up. The line was held until 5.00 pm, when the British retired 150 yards to an old trench. A large number of men had been killed or wounded along the line by machine guns. Amongst those killed in action was Vernon Alfred Clifton. He was 23; his little boy at home was 6.

But this was not the end of the bad news for Fanny Clifton during that terrible summer of 1915.

Vernon Alfred Clifton junior married Edith Mitchell in the Witney area in 1941, and died aged 67 in the Oxford area in 1975.

William Clifton
*10692 Private, 5th Battalion,
Oxfordshire & Buckinghamshire Light Infantry*
Northmoor

SEVEN WEEKS AFTER the death of his older brother Vernon, William Clifton died during a diversionary attack connected with that great killing field of 1915, the Battle of Loos.

William was born in Northmoor on 20th September 1896; his father Isaac was buried nine days later aged 41. The shock for his mother Fanny can only be imagined. She already had seven other children under 17 years old. As we have seen from the story of William's brother Vernon, she took work as a charwoman and set about making the best of things for her family at Clark's Cottage, even adding an illegitimate grandson to her list of responsibilities. By the age of 14, William was paying his own way by working as a farm labourer.

The 5th (Service) Battalion of the Ox & Bucks Light Infantry was formed at Oxford in August 1914. On 21st May 1915 they landed at Boulogne. On 19th September 1915 the whole of William's battalion had hot baths and a change of shirts in Poperinghe, followed by church parade at 11.30 am. Companies practised the attack on skeleton trenches in the afternoon.

Forty men of the battalion were allowed to go each night to the 6th Division 'Fancies', and forty to the cinema in Poperinghe. 'Fancies' were legalised brothels. The French thought nothing of allowing their soldiers to use brothels so, not wanting to offend their allies, the British High Command insisted that the Fancies should be kept 'in bounds' for most of the war. The brothels, along with cafés and bars, provided men with an escape from the slaughter and filth of the trenches. Separate establishments catered to officers and men, but all were bright and warm, light and jovial.

William Clifton and his comrades were briefed on the evening of 24th September 1915 that the following morning they were to attack German trenches in the vicinity of Hooge and Bellewaarde Lake. Crucially, the action was intended to divert attention and resources from a major attempt to break through at Loos. The preliminary bombardment was to open at 3.50 am, zero hour was fixed for 4.20 am. Steady rain meant that the men spent a miserable night in their wet clothes, waiting for dawn and for zero hour.

The Second Attack on Bellewaarde, as the action became known, turned out to be a disaster. Some objectives were reached, but the Germans evidently knew of the planned attack in advance, and the Ox & Bucks had to withdraw when the Germans counter-attacked.

Writing in the 5th Battalion's war diary, the Adjutant explains: 'The failure

Ooh la la: Soldiers on the Somme were permitted to visit 'Fancies', or licensed French brothels

of the Brigade to hold the line after it had been captured was due to our left column being almost wiped out by enemy artillery fire while lying out in the open prior to the assault. Possibly, enemy patrols had observed the gaps cut in our wire by which the left column was to go out; at any rate, they put all their guns on to this spot and scarcely shelled south of the Hedge Sap at all.

'Apparently, only two corporals were left to lead the attack, and about 20 men to see it through. These survivors were a good deal unnerved by the explosion of the mine close to them (under the enemy redoubt opposite Sunken Road), and when they started off they went too much to the left.

'The right column reached their objective, the enemy second line, and held it until forced back by a very strong counter-attack. Prisoners told us that they had been expecting our attack for three days, which accounts for the strength and rapidity of their counter-attack with fresh troops. The gap in our centre was fatal, and the enemy grasped that fact at once. As far as one could see, every German was armed with bombs.'

Out of 15 officers, the 5th Battalion lost 13, and out of 767 ranks, they lost 463, including William Clifton. He was five days past his nineteenth birthday.

Recruitment poster

Arthur Coles
*27137 Private, 6th Battalion,
Oxfordshire & Buckinghamshire Light Infantry*
Stanton Harcourt

BORN IN 1897 in Stanton Harcourt, Arthur Coles troubled the written record very little. But he would give his life at one of the most important turning points of the First World War.

In August 1917, the British Expeditionary Force conceived the idea of a series of large-scale attacks to secure a breakthrough of the German Hindenburg Line. Artillery, armour, aircraft and infantry would operate in concert in 'all-arms' battles. The German defences were formidable; Cambrai having been a quiet stretch of front thus far enabled the Germans to fortify their lines in depth and the British were aware of this. The opening of the Battle of Cambrai on 20th November 1917 is often identified as the first demonstration of the sophisticated techniques and technologies required to effect such a battle.

On that day, the British attack broke deeply and quickly into apparently impregnable defences with few casualties. This early result was widely regarded as being a great and spectacular achievement, so positive was it in comparison with the recent ghastly slog to Passchendaele. The end of the first day was even greeted in Britain by the ringing of church bells.

The massed use of tanks, despite being a further increase on previous deployments, was not entirely new but the success of the attack and the resulting Allied press enthusiasm, including in the United States, were unprecedented. The particular effectiveness of the tanks at Cambrai was the initial passage through barbed-wire defences, which had been previously supposed by the Germans to be impregnable. The notion that the Hindenburg Line was inviolable was exploded.

Ten days later, German reserves brought the advance to a halt. The German counter-attack showed the effectiveness of artillery, trench mortars and evolving stormtrooper tactics. By the end of the battle, the British retained some of the ground captured in the north and the Germans a smaller amount taken in the south.

In *Soldier from the Wars Returning* (Hutchinson & Co, 1965), author Charles Carrington reports the words of a former junior officer: 'Cambrai was a highly speculative gamble which I find inexplicable, so out of character is it with the rest of [Field Marshal Sir Douglas] Haig's career, not because it was inventive but because it was haphazard, not thought through.' The same officer went on that it was a 'harum-scarum affair, ill-planned and feebly directed, yet in military history it stands as the most significant battle of the First World War'.

The British reported losses of dead, wounded and missing of 44,207

A British tank blocking the canal crossing at Cambrai

between 20th November and 8th December. Of these, some 6,000 were taken prisoner in the enemy counterstroke on 30th November. Enemy casualties were estimated at approximately 45,000. These figures are still the subject of debate, but Cambrai was ultimately a disappointing exercise with a costly outcome. One of those relatively few casualties on the first day of the Cambrai Operations was Arthur Coles. He was killed in action on 20th November 1917, aged 20.

After Arthur's death his mother, Sarah Coles of Eaton, had his name listed on the memorial in the church at Stanton Harcourt. Arthur's grandmother, Elizabeth Alder, was a Stanton Harcourt girl, and there were still members of the Alder family in the village at the end of the war.

As for Sarah, the little riverside hamlet of Eaton where she lived on the Berkshire side of the Thames has no church or memorial of its own and, when the ferry was operating, it was just as easy to cross to the villages on the flat Oxfordshire bank as to toil up the slope to Appleton. Or perhaps she simply moved to Stanton Harcourt after the war.

The ferry at Bablock Hythe, pictured from the Berkshire bank c.1911

Dan Coombs
232480, Leading Seaman (Po), HM Submarine D3
Standlake

THE HISTORY OF Dan Coombs and his little sister Violet reveals something about the workhouse system at the turn of the twentieth century. Readers of the novels of Dickens and Hardy are accustomed to tragic souls going into such institutions generally never to emerge alive, but this was not the reality for many younger inmates. The vagaries of seasonal agricultural work or a sudden family catastrophe might oblige parents to park some of their offspring in the local workhouse simply to avoid starvation. But as soon as the crisis was past, parents would retrieve their children, and there is no reason to suppose that this ghastly cycle caused them any less anguish than it would modern families today.

Witney Union workhouse at Curbridge

Yew Tree Cottage

Dan's father William Coombs of Yew Tree Cottage, Standlake was facing an impossible situation. He had married local girl Martha Jane Green in 1882 and, working as a farm labourer, he supported a family of four girls and a boy. But after the youngest child Violet was born, his wife Martha died. This left William, a single man on a low wage, with four young children to care for and support – Mary Louisa, 8, Alice, 7, Dan 6, Daisy, 5, and baby Violet. It could not be done without some sort of help.

So in 1901 we find Dan, 11, and little Violet, 7, in the workhouse in Curbridge, where they would have been housed in separate wings for boys and girls. Inmates in the workhouse received free education, food and medical treatment. The Witney Union workhouse at Curbridge could accommodate 450, and a nearby quarry provided work for male inmates.

But conditions in the workhouse were harsh. Anxious to discourage 'idlers' and the lazy, the authorities ensured that the prospect of admission to such an institution was feared among potential inmates. Food was scarce and bland, discipline strict, and humiliating uniforms were imposed. The work required was supposed to act as a deterrent. Women found themselves cleaning, making beds, cooking, washing and sewing while the men were engaged in stone breaking, pumping water, milling corn, and grinding bones to make fertiliser.

Whilst it must have been a heart-breaking decision for William to send his children there, it was perhaps also a relief to know that they were receiving the basic necessities until they were old enough to begin working. Girls were usually then sent into service, boys often despatched straight into the army or navy.

Eldest sister Mary had already gone into service for the Moretons, a farming family in Cutteslowe. By 1911 Violet had returned home from the workhouse to look after her 53 year-old father. All the other children had left. Alice was in service for the owner of a boarding house in Hampstead.

On 12th March 1918 French airship *AT-0* was patrolling off Fécamp in the English Channel. At 2.20 pm a vessel was spotted to her north east. The airship drew closer for recognition purposes and, according to her commander, the submarine fired rockets at her. In fact, having identified French roundels on the aircraft, the officer of the watch on HM Submarine *D3* ordered that recognition rockets be fired to signal that they were a friendly vessel. Mistaking the rockets for aggressive fire, the airship bombed the submarine and raked the hull with gunfire. The submarine disappeared but several minutes later men were seen in the water.

The French airship cut its engines and began to descend in an effort to rescue the men. Without the noise of their engines they heard one of the submariners shout in English: 'You've got us!' The French realised their mistake and made frantic efforts to organise a rescue but, by the time a vessel did reach the area, the survivors had joined their comrades beneath the waves. Dan Coombs was 29.

In 1921 Violet married Standlake farm labourer William Knipe. He was the older brother of Archibald and Henry Knipe (see pages 107 and 110). Violet died in 1940.

The crew of HM Submarine D3

George Eaton

*T/202272 Private, 3rd/4th Battalion,
Queen's (Royal West Surrey) Regiment*
Standlake

THE EATONS OF STANDLAKE knew well the hazardous existence of babies living in poverty. According to a report in *Jackson's Oxford Journal* in 1900, George Eaton's mother Sarah testified in court that she had watched baby Bertie, born a healthy son of her neighbours William and Rachel Rose in Church End, ail and die in a few short weeks during that summer. William Rose earned only eleven shillings a week, and was considered an 'imbecile'; his wife Rachel was subject to fits.

In the circumstances, William was acquitted and Rachel sentenced to one day's imprisonment. The case may horrify us today, but it illustrates that the magistrates did attempt to modify punishment according to the mental and physical capabilities of the accused.

Unsurprisingly then, George's father Alfred was prepared to take his opportunities where he found them in order to support his family. George Richard Eaton was born in 1883, the son of Alfred Eaton, originally from Combe, and Sarah Ann Hanslow of Standlake. They married in December 1865, although Sarah already had a daughter, Elizabeth, about two years old. This does not preclude the possibility that Alfred Eaton was the child's father.

At the family home in Church End there were three more children – all sons: Alfred, James, and George. In fact, Sarah and Alfred had eight living babies altogether, so evidently some had either died in childhood or left home

Above: Church End, Standlake. Below: Mobilisation of George's regiment in August 1914

by 1911. Alfred was a carter when his children were small, then when his son James grew up they worked together on the roads. But in his old age, after James left home, Alfred switched to farm labouring.

Still using her mother's name Hanslow, Sarah's illegitimate daughter Elizabeth married in 1890 to Samuel Francis Barfoot, a street paviour employed by the Oxford Corporation. They lived Duke Street in New Botley.

George himself began his working life as a groom, but by his late twenties he was a bread baker. Or, at least, this was his aspiration; in fact, on the 1911 census return both George and his father Alfred confessed to being out of work. Then came the war, and for men of George's generation the problem of joblessness was removed.

George fought with the Queen's (Royal West Surrey) Regiment, sometimes called the 'Mutton Lancers' because of the lamb and flag emblem on their cap badges. The Queen's (Royal West Surrey) Regiment, with its depot in Guildford, contained seven battalions at the outset of the war. The 1st and 2nd Battalions comprised full-time professional soldiers and the 3rd Battalion was a 'special reserve unit', made up of part-time volunteer soldiers, some of whom were former regulars. They provided reinforcements to the first two battalions in the event of war.

On 9th August 1917 3rd/4th Battalion moved to France and plunged into the Third Battle of Ypres, otherwise known as Passchendaele. On 10th October the battalion war diary recorded a 'day devoted to rest and cleaning up'. Even so, four men were killed, and three men were wounded. Presumably occasional ordinance still affected the troops sporadically, or maybe snipers were ever-alert to their chances. George Eaton was one of the four killed on 10th October, eight weeks after arriving in France. He was 34.

George's father Alfred Eaton died aged 78 in 1920; his mother Sarah lived to the great age of 90, dying in 1930.

William Esson
Major, Royal Navy, Royal Marine Light Infantry
Northmoor

IF OUR PURPOSE is to remember in life the fallen of the Lower Windrush Valley, we must acknowledge that nobody can uphold heroic standards of behaviour every day, dawn till dusk, even an officer. Anyway, the fact that William Esson was cited as co-respondent in a grisly divorce case need not suggest that he was any less gentlemanly than the most humble farm-worker – merely that he came from a class which, in the event of domestic difficulty, had the resources to go to law to resolve the situation, and hence any proceedings were recorded for posterity.

William Esson was born in 1873, the son of Scots-born Oxford academic William Esson and his wife, former-governess Eliza Meek. He attended the Dragon School in Oxford. From there he went on to Rugby, and then in 1893

Dragon School, Oxford

he attended the Royal Naval College at Greenwich, joining the Royal Marine Light Infantry as second lieutenant aged 19. His brother James was at Malvern College; James was a Minor (junior) Scholar and School House Prefect, and a promising football-player. He left Malvern at Easter 1893. The boys had a sister, Margaret, who remained in the family home in Bradmore Road, Oxford, where later in 1893 Eliza Esson died aged 51. In the following year, James died at the age of 19. It must have been a gloomy period in the Esson household.

In July 1900 William was promoted from first lieutenant and, at 27, he was captain of the twin-screw cruiser HMS *Hyacinth*, then docked at Devonport. While based at the Royal Marine barracks at Forton in Alverstoke, Hampshire, William became involved with the wife of Hugh Robert Fowler, a retired army officer and local businessman supplying materials to the shipbuilding trade. In 1901 Fowler is described on the census as 'in Africa overseeing brick business and farm'. By 1908, William was cited co-respondent in Fowler's divorce from his wife Minnie Louisa, hardly a development designed to please his father, by now Savilian Professor of Geometry at Merton. Newspaper coverage dragged on for five years.

And then at last William's situation, the irregularity of which must have caused his father some distress, was resolved. In 1913, *The Times* was able to announce the marriage of 'Major W Esson RMLI to Mrs M L Fowler of Manor House, Northmoor, Oxon'. However, William and Minnie do not appear to have lived much in Northmoor (if at all), spending their short married life at Bridge House in the Botley Road, now the River Hotel.

Following the Gallipoli campaign, William's ship HMS *Russell* was the last battleship of the British Dardanelles Squadron to leave the area. After the contribution which *Russell* gave in the Dardanelles, the Admiralty felt that she and her crew merited a short rest in Malta. But it was not to be.

Early on the morning of 27th April 1916, William was off-duty in his cabin. HMS *Russell* was just four miles out from the Grand Harbour in Malta when she hit a mine. She struck a second, then a third explosion occurred. The ship remained afloat for about twenty minutes before capsizing. Of the 720 crew,

William Esson: a captain in the Royal Marine Light Infantry before the war

Above: After her divorce, Minnie Fowler appears to have moved to Northmoor Manor

Left: Bridge House, Botley Road, Oxford

124 lost their lives, including half the ship's complement of officers. William's cabin was immediately over the site of the first explosion; he was never seen again. William Esson was 42.

Minnie Esson fled back to London where she died aged 67 in 1940. She never remarried.

George Herbert Florey
*115 Guardsman, 4th Battalion,
Guards Machine Gun Regiment*
Standlake

IT IS TEMPTING to think of the boys and men who went abroad from the Lower Windrush Valley as wide-eyed and unworldly. But the Floreys of Standlake were enterprising businessmen with commercial links as far away as London.

Between 1873 and 1879 British agriculture had suffered from wet summers that damaged grain crops. The poor harvests, however, masked a greater threat to British agriculture: growing imports of foodstuffs from abroad. The development of the steam ship and extensive railway networks in Britain and the USA allowed US farmers with much larger and more productive farms to export hard grain to Britain at a price that undercut British farmers.

Once the railway network was established, many British farming families responded by creating outlets for their produce in a rapidly-expanding capital. Every day, vast quantities of grain, milk, and cheese were moved from the countryside to London to feed a hungry population. The Floreys of Standlake were not the sort of businessmen to miss out on such an opportunity.

During the late 1800s, both before and after his marriage, George Herbert Florey's father Mark spent a few years working with George's uncle Thomas at their establishment in the Old Kent Road in Deptford. The men acted as agents selling the corn produced in the family's fields at home in Oxfordshire.

Mark Florey came home to marry George's mother Anne Shepherd from

Above: Florey Farm in Brighthampton, one of several acquired by the family over the years. *Below:* Old Kent Road, home of the Floreys' London outpost

Ducklington in March 1884, but he soon carried his new wife off back to the city and the couple's first three sons – James, Walter, and Milton – were born in London. It seems that Mark and Anne moved between Standlake and the Old Kent Road over the next few years as Mark continued to represent the family business in London.

As a family man, Mark was by 1897 in a separate tenement at 298 Old Kent Road, while his uncle Thomas remained at number 825. Back in Standlake there came Percy, George, Edith, Henry, Arthur, Hilda, Ethel and, finally, Norman. Percy, Henry, and Arthur died as infants, leaving five sons and three daughters running round the farmhouse in Standlake main street. Perhaps the family home in Oxfordshire where George Herbert grew up, with its squealing children and the squealing piglets of their father's prize-winning pigs, was only marginally less noisy than the Old Kent Road.

George was in the 4th Company, Guards Machine Gun Regiment. The regiment was formed in 1915 at a time when machine-gun companies were beginning to be introduced into the Guards Division. In April 1917, four companies merged to form the Machine Gun Guards.

George died of his wounds on 6th September 1917 during the Third Battle of Ypres ('Passchendaele'). He was 24.

His brother Milton enlisted as a gunner with the Royal Garrison Artillery in April 1915. At the Battle of Lys in April 1918 Milton suffered serious gunshot wounds to his back, shoulder and left leg, but he survived to return home to Standlake. He was described on his discharge papers as 'a sober, hardworking man'.

In fact, nine out of ten men came back from the war, but that does not necessarily mean they came home healthy. The physical and mental effects stayed with many veterans for the rest of their lives.

George's sister Edith married Josiah Southorn in 1914. His mother Ann died in 1938 aged 78. Ethel married Thomas Tanner in 1939. Father Mark Florey died in 1952 aged 91.

Percy John Franklin

*10675 Lance Corporal, 5th Battalion,
Oxfordshire & Buckinghamshire Light Infantry*
Stanton Harcourt

THE TRAGEDY OF Percy John Franklin is that a description of his life before the war fits into a single paragraph. Born on 9th March 1897 at Payne's Farm, West End, Percy was the seventh chid and first surviving son of farmer William Franklin and his wife Alice Godfrey of Appleton. John, as he was

Payne's Farm, West End

Alice Franklin with baby Percy John on her lap

known at home, left school at around 13 and then, after helping his father on the farm for a while, he moved to Witney to take up an apprenticeship with a butcher.

At the outbreak of war in August 1914, John signed up to serve with the 5th Battalion, Ox & Bucks, part of Lord Kitchener's New Army. Writing home from Aldershot on 9th May 1915, John revealed that his letter may be the last for some time as he will sail in a couple of weeks, though he doesn't know where he will be sent.

On 19th June, under heavy fire from German shrapnel and gas shells, John's battalion went into trenches in Railway Wood near Ypres. Low-lying ground was thickly covered with gas fumes, which made breathing difficult and the eyes smart painfully. The battalion returned from the front line on the 20th June.

On 8th July the battalion returned to the trenches at Railway Wood. Two days later John was wounded; the regiment's war diary states that: 'At 7.10 am the enemy bombarded our railway barricade and knocked it down. About 100 heavy-explosive shells were fired at it. A great deal of artillery fire on both sides all day, also trench mortars firing at Railway Wood. Casualties: 7 wounded.' John returned to take part in a planned diversionary attack to the Battle of Loos.

On 16th of August John wrote his last-known letter home to his sister 'Bess' (see opposite). On 19th September the whole battalion received hot baths and clean shirts in Poperinghe, followed by church parade at 11.30 am.

Battalion orders for 23rd September place John's company leaving the Menin Gate at about 7.40 pm via Menin Road and Cambridge Road and marching out to the trenches. It is possible that John was one of eighteen men from C Company attached to B Company as a wiring party.

C Company were to dig out the international trench and furnish working parties to carry up bombs, tools, water, ammunition, sand bags and rations. The battalion was to be in position at midnight on 24th September 1915. The attack began with an artillery bombardment at 3.50 am on 25th, and then a mine exploding at 4.19 am was the sign for the assault to commence, giving the British an hour to try and pin down as many German troops as possible before the main attack commenced at Loos at 6.30 am.

The 5th Ox & Bucks quickly gained their allotted targets. At about 5.00 am Private H R Brooks of C Company saw John in a German communication trench at Bellewaarde Farm on his way back to the British lines. He was wounded in the arm, but not severely. This is the last reported sighting of Percy John Franklin. He was 18 years old.

The objectives were held for a few hours but the 5th Ox & Bucks were pushed back at around 8.00 am. Out of 782 officers and men there were 467 killed, died of wounds, wounded or missing. John's body was never found.

Although Alice Franklin knew that her son was missing in action, she did not learn the terrible truth until a year after John's death. When she died in 1921, John's medals (1915 Star, Victory medal, and British War medal), were buried with her at Northmoor.

Percy John Franklin's last-known letter home

Henry Arthur Green
8060 Private, 3rd Battalion, Oxfordshire & Buckinghamshire Light Infantry
Standlake

THE GREENS AND the Busbys would appear to have been among the most unassuming possible of families working the land of the Lower Windrush Valley at the turn of the twentieth century. In fact, they were part of a quiet rebellion.

Henry Green's father William married Jane Busby of Northmoor in September 1868. A dash of independent thought in their make-up had persuaded the two families to abandon the Church of England and embrace Methodism. This was a religious strain of thought developed in the previous century by Oxford don John Wesley. An emphasis on equality among worshippers and an active approach towards the care of the poor and sick appealed to humble agricultural workers battling to survive in a difficult world. Its preachers emerged from among its own ranks, rather than from the hushed cloisters of the University where Church of England clergy lived lives of relative luxury compared with the members of their flocks.

Henry's maternal grandfather James Busby was the minister to Northmoor, living at the Primitive Methodist Chapel in Chapel Lane. Along with him lived his daughters Mary Ann and Jane and his sons George and Emanuel. When William Green married the minister's daughter Jane, he too moved into the household, and there the couple had their two first children, William James and Charles Thomas. George and Sophia arrived while the Greens were still

The site of the Primitive Methodist Chapel in Chapel Lane, Northmoor

in Northmoor, but Henry Arthur – 'Harry' – came along only after the family had moved to Allotment Lane in Standlake.

Like all the men of the Green family, once his schooldays were over Harry took up farm work. His sister Sophia had married during the spring of 1906, and his father died soon after, but luckily for the newly-widowed Jane she still had her sons George and Harry at home with her. Not for long, however.

At 23 years old in August 1911, Henry enlisted with the 5th (Reserve) Battalion, Ox & Bucks Light Infantry. He had already served as an irregular with the Royal Artillery and the Royal Field Artillery, so he was immediately called up from the reserves in August 1914, but soon conditions in the trenches began to take their toll.

In France in November 1914 he began to experience pain which gradually worsened to the point where he had 'very little control over [his] right leg and can only hobble along with the aid of a stick'. A medical report dated March 1916 states that severe sciatica has rendered Henry totally incapacitated. The report confirms that this disability is 'probably permanent' and the 'result of active service'.

Conditions in the trenches

The Primitive Methodist Chapel on The Green in Standlake

Recruitment poster

COME LAD SLIP ACROSS AND HELP

Harry came home and in 1917 he married Mary Louisa Coombs, sister of Dan Coombs (see page 67). The groom was 31 and poorly, the bride was 30 and facing a life of domestic service. The alliance reflected a tradition of friendship and intermarriage between the Coombs and Green families, but the happy resolution of the practical problems of Harry's care and Mary Louisa's declining prospects as a single woman cannot be denied. Also, Mary Louisa was pregnant. On 22nd February 1917 she had a son called William.

In the following year Harry finally succumbed to his injuries, dying in December aged 32.

James H Green

201063 Lance Corporal,
1st/4th Oxfordshire & Buckinghamshire Light Infantry
Standlake

ANOTHER GREEN FAMILY lived in Standlake at this time, but they were unrelated to Harry Green's clan. James's father, also named James, was a shepherd from Kintbury in Berkshire. James's mother was wheelwright's daughter Minnie Crook from Ramsbury in Wiltshire. In 1893 the couple married and decided to leave the land and move to London to find work.

James senior took up a position as a stonemason's labourer, while Minnie raised her young family of seven children at their home in Henry Street in Lambeth (two had died). In the rapidly growing city, and with the proximity of the Archbishop of Canterbury's great, medieval stone palace at Lambeth, there must have been plenty of opportunities for stone workers.

Born in London in September 1896, James was the second surviving child and the elder of two boys. He grew up surrounded by five sisters: Beatrice, Gertrude, Hilda, Winifred and Agnes. Agnes died aged 7 in 1907, and little Victor arrived in the following year.

By the time James was 14 years old, James Green senior had moved his family to Rack End, Standlake. Quite why the Greens would move from an area offering plentiful work to a tiny village in Oxfordshire is a puzzle. Perhaps by his forties, James was beginning to feel the effects of years of breathing in the dust of hewn stone, and felt the country air would be better for his lungs.

Evidently James senior decided that a return to shepherding would be

Lambeth High Street

taking pastoralism too far because by 1911 he was putting his stone-wrangling skills to use mending the roads. Most country people moved from place to place using footpaths; hard roads and lanes were generally for use by horses, carts, and waggoners. Before the widespread use of tarmacadam, local stone was simply crushed and packed into the mud. Just like today, constant repair of potholes would be necessary. Up until 1894, this work was overseen by an elected amateur, the Surveyor of Highways or 'Waywarden'. Following the Local Government Act of 1894, responsibility for roads was removed from the parish and transferred to rural or county councils.

At 14, James junior took to more traditional local work as a farm labourer.

James Green's father turned his hand to road mending

James Green rose to Lance Corporal with the 1st/4th Ox & Bucks. He died in an attack on Ronssoy on the Western Front on 5th April 1917 during the German retreat to the Hindenburg Line.

Winifred Green married Arthur Capel in 1910 and died in the Oxford area in 1972. Gertrude married 'cycle enameller' John Groves in 1916. A James Green of around the right age to be James junior's father died in the Witney area aged 59 in 1925.

James's youngest brother Victor endured horrors of his own. Having married in 1930, Victor went off to fight in the Second World War with the Royal Artillery. He was taken prisoner and put to work on the infamous Burma-to-Siam railway, built by the Empire of Japan to support its forces in the Burma campaign. About 61,000 Allied prisoners of war were subjected to forced labour during its construction, and more than 12,000 died, including Victor. (The proportion of deaths among South East Asian civilians subject to forced labour was even higher.) In addition to malnutrition and physical abuse, malaria, cholera, dysentery and tropical ulcers were common contributing factors in the death of workers on the Burma railway.

Victor died at Tonchan South camp in Thailand on 1st July 1943. He was 35.

Thomas Hudson
21913 Guardsman, 3rd Battalion, Coldstream Guards
Stanton Harcourt

YOU HAVE TO ADMIRE the chutzpah of the farmboy who applies for, and gets, a posting in the élite Coldstream Guards, the oldest regiment in the regular army in continuous active service. Thomas was a carter, born in June 1894 the son of Frederick Hudson, one of the many men employed as gardeners in Stanton Harcourt – tending the grounds perhaps at Parsonage House, or more likely the Manor.

Thomas's mother, Deddington-born Emily Ada Seeney, was the daughter of an engineer/smith in a factory. The factory was possibly that of the Mason family, recorded as locksmiths and ironmongers from the late 17th century. Mason's factory was a considerable employer in late nineteenth-century Deddington. The Mason family established an axletree factory in around 1820, and the firm exported its products widely overseas. It was reputed to have supplied axles for the royal coaches.

In 1911 Thomas's sisters Edith, 21, and Evelyn, 20, had gone into service. Edith was general servant to a clergyman and his wife in Thame, and Evelyn was general servant to an elderly couple in Oxford. At 16 Thomas was working as a carter on a farm, and his younger brother Henry, 13, was a ploughboy. Evidently there was insufficient money to keep Henry in school. There was a long gap before the final child, Christopher, who was born in 1907.

Thomas Hudson travelled to Birmingham to enlist in the Coldstream Guards. Because the regiment entered the service of the Crown after the 1st

The village of Stanton Harcourt

Regiment of Foot Guards, it was placed second in seniority in terms of the Household Troops. The regiment responded to this calumny by adopting the motto *Nulli Secundus* (Second to None) because the Coldstream Guards is older than the senior regiment. The regiment always stands on the left of the line when on parade with the rest of the Foot Guards, so standing 'second to none'.

On 30th November 1917, the 1st Guards Brigade set off for Gouzeaucourt. Whilst the tanks were getting underway, Brigadier General Champion de Crespigny of 1st Guards Brigade had already ridden forward from Metz to discover that Gouzeaucourt was held by the Germans.

Without artillery or tank support the General deployed his men and attacked the village down the Metz–Gouzeaucourt Road – the 1st Irish Guards north of the road and the 2nd and 3rd Coldstreams to the south.

Their deployment had been masked by the crest of the hill just to the west of the village and, as they came into sight of the German troops, they were met with machine-gun and artillery fire. Their own machine-gun crews subdued

The village of Gouzeaucourt after the fighting

the enemy, and the Guardsmen stormed in to retake the village. By 1.30 pm the Guards were on the eastern edge of the village and numerous guns that had been abandoned a few hours ago were now brought back into action against the retreating Germans. By the time the tanks arrived, they found that the job had been done without them.

At 5.30 am on 1st December 1917, the 3rd Coldstream Guards attacked Quentin Mill. The attack stalled when they were fired on by machine guns in an old British trench called Green Switch, in front of which was a previously unknown belt of wire. Two-thirds of the Guardsmen were hit.

Thomas Hudson died of his wounds on 1st December 1917. He was 23.

In 1939 Thomas's spinster sister Edith was sharing a house in Circus Street off the Cowley Road, and working as a domestic cleaner. She died in September 1981 aged 91.

E B Johnson
50440 Private, 4th Battalion, Worcestershire Regiment
Standlake

THE JOHNSON FAMILY of Cote near Standlake, seemingly unrelated to the Standlake Johnsons of engineering fame, give us an unexpected glimpse into the lives of the commercial classes of Oxford and Witney at the turn of the twentieth century. For, though Edwin Bertie Johnson was born the son of a farmer in 1899, the Johnsons originally made their money in retail.

Edwin's grandfather Thomas Johnson was actually an Oxford draper who started off in premises opposite Carfax Tower at 5 Queen Street, living above the shop with his first wife Elizabeth and two assistants. In 1867 an unpleasant

Queen Street in Oxford

incident took place in the shop which illustrates that some things don't change.

According to a court report in *Jackson's Oxford Journal* dated 8th June 1867, on 3rd June Sarah Ayres of Headington Quarry had gone into Johnson's shop claiming she wanted to buy both a hat and a feather. She was conducted upstairs by an assistant to choose the feather from a box. When she had gone downstairs again, it was noticed that a second feather worth a shilling was missing. No master-criminal, Ayres denied having the feather, 'but opened her pocket and disclosed the missing article'. Taking into account Sarah's youth and previous good character, the mayor and aldermen sentenced Sarah to three days' imprisonment.

Elizabeth Johnson gave birth to twin sons, Edwin's father Thomas Bertie and William Percy, in 1868. She died two years later – perhaps in childbirth once more. When the twins were 11, their widowed father Thomas Johnson married his housekeeper Ada Habbijam. (That interesting name Habbijam rejoices in origins which are Norman-French, meaning a maker of sleeveless mail armour.) Edwin's father Thomas Bertie was packed off to Howard House school in Thame. Thomas senior and Ada eventually retired via George Street to a handsome, double-fronted villa on the corner of Walton Well Road in Oxford, currently home to Thomas Merrifield estate agents.

Edwin's father Thomas Bertie Johnson married butcher's daughter Ada Fowler from West End in Witney in early 1890. Evidently sufficient wealth had been accumulated to establish Thomas Bertie in farming, first at Clements Field Farm, Shores Green, Cogges, then at Cote Farm. Thomas and Ada had six children: Gladys Irene, Reginald John Cyril, Ruby Brangwin, Edwin Bertie, Ada Elizabeth Evelyn, and Percy Dodwell. Also living in the household was a mother's help to ease Ada's load.

By 1911, 19 year-old Gladys was living in Witney with the Cook family and working as a draper's clerk for the head of the family William Henry Cook who dealt in general drapery, clothes and household furnishings from his premises in Market Square. Seventeen year-old Reginald was boarding with widow Minnie Jones at Woodgreen in Witney and working as a sorting clerk

Cote Farm, where Edwin Johnson grew up

and telegraphist, presumably at the post office. An apprenticeship had been secured for 15 year-old Ruby with Witney draper George Wickham. At 12, Edwin was still in school. In 1913 Gladys would marry John Hudson, a clerk for one of the blanket manufacturers.

Edwin joined 4th Battalion, Worcestershire Regiment. During the early months of 1918 the 4th Battalion was active in the Lys Valley. The Battle of the Lys (7th–29th April 1918) was also known as the Lys Offensive, or the Fourth Battle of Ypres. Perhaps this is where Edwin sustained the wounds which eventually caused his death on 20th June 1918. He was 19.

Ruby Johnson married Herbert Saunders in Headington in 1920. Ada Johnson died unmarried in the Witney area aged 73 in 1940. Edwin's father Thomas Bertie Johnson died in 1950, leaving over £6,000 in his will. Reginald became a farmer and died in 1965 aged 72; Percy Johnson became an electrician and married Winifred Devonshire in 1942. He died in West Oxfordshire in 1988 aged 87.

James T Johnson
9860 Lance Corporal, 2nd Battalion,
Oxfordshire & Buckinghamshire Light Infantry
Standlake

IT MAY HAVE BEEN with some trepidation that, in the winter of 1873, Standlake carpenter James Johnson married the daughter of a man who described himself as a 'castrator'. Ann Coleing's father was a pig dealer from a widespread local clan of butchers. Ann and James set up home at Bay Tree Cottage, Standlake and had four surviving daughters and one son. That son was James T Johnson, known in the family as 'Thomas' and born in Standlake in December 1888, the youngest surviving child of five, and with four sisters.

Bay Tree Cottage

Box Villa in Charlton on Otmoor

Photo courtesy Nigel Lambert

Thomas's eldest sister Annie introduced a trace of the Continental into the Johnson family in 1896 by marrying a Viennese waiter called Jacques John Saxl, known as 'John'. Annie had probably met Saxl while in service in Bethnal Green. Annie and John set up home in Crown Hill Road in Willesden and produced a brood of six children. In the spring of 1911, Annie and her tribe – aged from 12 years down to a babe-in-arms – descended on the Johnsons in Standlake, and 23 year-old Thomas promptly made his exit.

Escaping the chaos at home, Thomas headed for Charlton on Otmoor where he stayed with a branch of the Honours, a well-established farming family, in their home at Box Villa. Head of the household James Honour was a 'hayter', or hay binder and dealer. Animals needed feeding all year round, and the new railway station a mile north of the village would have enabled Mr Honour to despatch fodder to a capital city powered largely by horses.

But Thomas's connection with the Honours was through another member of the household. James Honour's daughter Elsie was married to a Standlake carpenter, Herbert Brusker, evidently an acquaintance of Thomas's. Thomas himself did not at this point follow his father's trade of carpentry; he worked as a painter. Insufficient work in a country village would oblige tradesmen like Thomas to travel to the jobs, and this may be the reason for his visit to Charlton on Otmoor.

However, another attraction in the Honour household was Elsie's elder sister, Fencott-born Florence, a dressmaker. Two years after the 1911 visit, Thomas and Florence were married in Standlake in March 1913. Florence gave birth to a daughter named Lilian Bessie in May 1914. But the young couple's plans for their life and family together were soon interrupted.

Thomas's service number suggests that he may have joined up with the Ox & Bucks Light Infantry in the early days of the war. The battalions of the Ox & Bucks on the Western Front saw extensive service during the Battle of the Somme (1st July–18th November), suffering heavily. On 28th July

Multi-storey town stabling for horses, essential to power turn-of-the-century London

The road to Waterlot Farm, scene of intense fighting in 1916

1916 the 2nd Ox & Bucks moved to front-line trenches near Waterlot Farm and sustained heavy casualties at the battle there on 30th July. James Thomas Johnson was killed in action on 30th July 1916, aged 28.

Thomas's wife Florence returned to her own family in Charlton on Otmoor, presumably taking little Bessie with her. Members of the Honour family still live in the village today.

In May 1923, at a time when a German accent may not have served as a social asset in England, Thomas's Viennese brother-in-law John Saxl and his 21 year-old son Francis departed on the *President Adams* for New York. John is described on the passenger manifest as a produce merchant and Francis as an electrical engineer. Whether or not the trip was an attempt at emigration, Francis was back in England when his death at 32 was registered in Witney in 1934. In 1942 John Saxl died there too, aged 68. Thomas's sister Annie followed in 1966 at the age of 90.

Harry Kelly

*10786 Corporal, C Company, 5th Battalion,
Oxfordshire & Buckinghamshire Light Infantry*
Northmoor

BORN IN 1881, Harold Thomas Kelly had already travelled throughout England by the time he settled with his parents on Pinnocks Farm in Northmoor. Following a career as an Inland Revenue inspector, Harry's father Thomas had retired to the county of his birth, Oxfordshire.

Thomas Kelly's work had obliged him to move his growing family around the country, from Gloucestershire to Yorkshire, from Staffordshire to London. Thomas's wife Sarah gave birth to her first child in Chipping Campden,

Pinnocks Farm

Before coming to Northmoor, the Kellys lived in this smart villa in Clapham

the next three, including Harry, in Cleckheaton, Yorkshire, and her fifth in Tipton, Staffordshire. Before coming to Northmoor, the family lived in a smart Victorian villa in Stormont Road leading to Clapham Common.

Harry appears to have harboured no ambition to follow his father into the Inland Revenue because, in 1911, he and his younger brother Aubrey were helping their father on the farm. Thomas Kelly was already in his late sixties, so it seems likely that his boys did most of the heavy work. And Kelly senior may already have been ailing; a move to the countryside was often deemed desirable for the health of an invalid. Eldest brother Denzil had married in 1907 and worked as a brewer's traveller (i.e. salesman) in Lancashire.

Although not directly involved in the severe fighting in the Somme, the towns of Arras, Achicourt, Ronville, St Saveur, Tilloy, Dainville, Faubourg d'Amiens, and Saint Catherine were coming under attack on a daily basis in the spring and early summer of 1916. Aeroplanes and observation balloons were used in concert with rifle fire and trench mortars to attack the trenches, headquarters, working parties, supply lines and observation posts on either side. Even so, the area was considered quiet.

The 5th Ox & Bucks war diary reads: 'Whilst in the trenches every one fed exceedingly well, the cookers being kept at Ronville or at Achicourt, according to which section of the line we were holding, and the men getting four meals a day. Except for an occasional strafe, the Hun kept remarkably quiet. We were told that when the French held this line there was a sort of compact between them and the Germans; at any rate, each side was protected by solid wire, on stout wooden posts, to a depth of 30 yards to the front. To find such a mass of wire was rather a surprise to us, as in the Salient wire 3 yards deep was considered by no means bad. Alas! with the arrival of Lewis guns, this beautiful wire got fearfully knocked about, as it became a regular practice to shoot them off from our parapet, and so cut the wire to ribbons, which meant endless wiring parties and a great waste of labour, until it was put a stop to.

'At first we used to be billeted in Arras and Simencourt, afterwards Bernville was substituted for the latter, and the transport camp was at one or the other of these two villages. In Arras two companies and HQ were billeted in the Ecole des Jeunes Filles, which was a most comfortable place; and the HQ Mess was in a big house close by, where the people were very kind, and often served us with most tasty dishes. One Company and its HQ was in the Commercial Hotel, and another was not far off.

'While in Arras itself we had practically no experience of shelling, and even in the line we had remarkably few casualties. June was a glorious month as far as the weather was concerned, although there were a few wet days. Life went on much as usual; the Battalion was in and out of the trenches; the enemy's shelling increased somewhat.'

One of those few casualties was Harry Kelly. He died at Ronville on 16th June 1916. He was 35. His mother had only just had to deal with the loss of her husband. Harry's father Thomas died in March 1915 at 72. Sarah moved to the village of Stonesfield near Woodstock, where she died in 1927 aged 77. Aubrey died in the Witney area in 1950, and Denzil died in Manchester in 1960.

George James Kensett
136074 Serjeant, 52nd Battalion, Canadian Infantry
(Manitoba Regiment)
Northmoor

AS A MEMBER of a Canadian infantry regiment, George James Kensett seems at first sight an exotic creature to find listed on the Northmoor war memorial. However, his story reveals how mobile and opportunist normal working families could be at this early point in the twentieth century.

In fact George was born in London in 1893, the son of labourer James George Kensett and Mary Clarke. George had two younger brothers, Henry and Sydney, and a sister, Ellen. In about 1912, lured by the promise of a

Kingwood Road in Fulham, where George Kensett grew up

Wilton Avenue on the right, at the junction with Jarvis Street in Toronto

better life abroad, the Kensett family emigrated from their flat in Kingwood Road in Fulham to Toronto in Canada. Over a period of one year, all three Kensett boys signed up from their home in Wilton Avenue with the Canadian Expeditionary Force. Leaving behind life as a dairyman (what we would call a milkman), George enlisted in the 74th Battalion in July 1915, Henry in the 169th in January 1916, and Sydney in the 201st in July of the same year.

George was promoted serjeant in the 52nd Battalion (Manitoba Regiment). Within days of arriving aboard a cattle-boat in France in February 1916, the 52nd moved to the front, and found itself thrust into battle at the Kemmel sector in early March of that year. Over the next three years the Canadians took part in relentless fighting. Survivors told stories of rat-infested trenches, sleepless nights on ground sheets under a single blanket, and ineffective rifles. One soldier even recalled walking to the front minus helmet or gas mask, having been told to pick them up along the way from the casualties.

The 52nd had a reputation for independence and audacity. Private W C Millar recalled their encounter with the Imperial Grenadier Guards on a narrow road in the Ypres sector: 'When seeing a bunch of mud-stained, unwashed Canadians coming along, the serjeant-major in charge of the Guards shouted out, in a voice which only an Imperial serjeant-major can assume, "Make way for the Guards! Make way for the Guards!" Our lieutenant who, I have no doubt, was seeing visions of a talk and possibly a bottle of champagne when we reached our billets, refused to be impressed and made this characteristic reply: "To H—l with the Guards! Carry on, Fifty-second!" Needless to state, the 52nd carried on and, for once in their lives, the Guards took the side of the road for the Canadians.'

Meanwhile, Norah Jane Busby of Chapel Lane in Northmoor was in service with the Cook family in Stanton Harcourt. She decided to strike out into the world, and found a place in Ealing, west London. When George was passing through England in February 1918 on his way to France, he and Norah were married.

During the Battle of Amiens just under six months later, on the morning of 13th August 1918 at Damery on the Somme, an aeroplane dropped a bomb and George was killed.

George's mother Mary Kensett lost all three of her sons within five months. Sydney was a private in the 19th Canadian Infantry Battalion when he died of his wounds on 23rd June 1918. Influenza carried off Henry three days after Armistice Day. The Spanish influenza pandemic, which affected the whole world and scourged Europe between 1918 and 1919, killed more people than the war itself.

Mary died in Toronto ten years later at 67. Her husband James, who had also served and been wounded in action, died in 1930 from angina. In 1921 their only surviving child, Ellen, married Sidney Sluce, himself a veteran of the war.

Back in Northmoor, poor little Norah Busby Kensett never experienced the excitement of a new life in Canada. She remarried in 1920, and some people still living in Northmoor at the time of writing will remember her and her husband Horace Janaway Bint. Norah died in 1970, Horace in 1994.

Archibald James Knipe
16312 Private, 1st Battalion, Royal Hampshire Regiment
Standlake

WHEN ARCHIBALD KNIPE'S parents John and Sarah married in the spring of 1883, the collective eyebrows of Standlake may have been ever-so-slightly raised. The bride was seven years older than the groom; she was also very obviously pregnant. Sarah had been married before, and brought with her to the Knipe home in Rack End a daughter, Ada Douglas, aged 9, and a son, Percival Douglas, aged 3.

John, an agricultural labourer, and Sarah had six surviving children of their own at regular two-year intervals: John (born a few weeks after his parents' marriage), William, Mary, Archibald, Henry, and George. Money had always been scarce – in fact, John had been prosecuted for poaching three years into his marriage. He was fined ten shillings – almost a week's wages. With a growing family to feed, this may not have been John's only foray beyond the bounds of the game laws, just the one where he got caught.

This lack of funds also meant that all the Douglas and Knipe offspring were sent out to work pretty early. Any schooling Percival Douglas enjoyed was over by the time he was 13; he was already working as a farm labourer. William Knipe was a groom at 15.

Archibald initially enlisted with the Ox & Bucks Light Infantry. But in May 1915 he was transferred to the Hampshire Regiment, probably to make up for losses in action.

The first day of the Battle of the Somme has become infamous for the

The Hampshires prepare to go over the top on the first day of the Battle of the Somme

largest number of deaths ever sustained in one day by the British Army. The battle was pre-empted by a week-long artillery bombardment of the German lines with 1,738,000 shells. The logic was that the artillery guns would destroy the German trenches as well as the barbed wire in front them. In fact, the Germans had prepared deep dugouts and all they had to do when

German prisoners bringing in the British wounded

the bombardment started was to move into the relative safety of the dugouts. When the bombardment stopped, the Germans would have known that this was the signal for an infantry advance. They planned then to emerge from the safety of their dugouts and man their machine guns to face the British and French.

On the morning of 1st July 1916 British and German troops faced each other in trenches separated by only a few hundred yards of 'no-man's land'. After another massive artillery bombardment the whistles blew and 100,000 men went over the top to attack the German trenches. The battalion war diary sums up the dreadful day in a few sentences:

'Great Offensive begins: at 7.30 am the whole line assaulted… As soon as our troops left the trenches heavy machine gun fire was brought to bear on them from all directions and it was impossible even to reach the German front line. Our casualties in officers amounted to 100 per cent and was also very heavy in other ranks. After lying about in shell-holes all day the men came back to their original front line.'

British soldiers were mown down in their thousands by machine-gun and artillery fire. Several truces were negotiated in order to recover the wounded from no-man's land. The British Army took 57,470 casualties, of which 19,240 men were killed. Archibald Knipe was among the dead, killed for the sake of an Allied gain of three square miles of territory. He was 21.

The generals had intended that the Battle of the Somme would hasten a victory for the Allies. But 1st July 1916 launched 141 days of horror. By November 1916 more than three million men had fought on the Somme and one million men were wounded or killed, making it one of the bloodiest battles in history.

Henry Knipe

10876 Lance Corporal, 5th Battalion, Oxfordshire & Buckinghamshire Light Infantry
Standlake

AS WE HAVE SEEN, even within the tiny Lower Windrush Valley there were parents who had to endure the unimaginable agony of the loss of more than one son in World War I. Henry ('Harry') Knipe died eight weeks after his elder brother Archibald (see page 107).

Henry enlisted with the Ox & Bucks Light Infantry and in August 1916 his battalion was ordered to make an assault on Delville Wood on the Somme. The battalion war diary paints a vivid picture of the start of the action: 'Two hours before the time for attack, which was 5.45 pm, the heavy artillery opened. It turned the wood into a perfect hell. I saw the beginning of it. Trees were flying about like matches, and great columns of earth were thrown up.'

Over 24th–25th August the 5th Battalion lost 44 men killed, 118 wounded, and 14 missing. Just over eight weeks after the death of his brother Archibald, Henry Knipe was killed in action on 24th August 1916 aged 24.

The poverty afflicting families like the Knipes of Standlake contributed to War Office thinking on the tricky subject of what to do with the mortal remains of British and Commonwealth servicemen killed overseas. Once the magnitude of the number of casualties to be expected began to become clear, the War Office took the decision not to repatriate bodies, but to bury men as close as possible to where they died.

It was decided that individual families' requests to have loved ones returned would be denied. Up until that point, families with the financial means to arrange for bodies to be returned home could do so. There was some resistance to this change in policy, especially among more well-to-do families, but it was decided that officers should remain beside their soldiers in the new graveyards. Orders were given that no bodies were to be exhumed and repatriated to Britain. They were to be taken to specially appointed graveyards; a photograph was then taken of the gravestone and sent to the family with instructions on how to locate the grave.

But relatives living on limited means could not dream at that time of visiting graves as far afield as France, Belgium, Greece, or even Mesopotamia. They required a focus for remembrance near to home, as well as a public acknowledgement within their own communities of the sacrifice their families had made. This is why men were commemorated in villages and towns throughout the United Kingdom as well as near the battlefield.

Archibald and Henry's troublesome brother George Knipe signed up with the Army Cyclist Corps in August 1914, giving as his occupation at the time 'carter'. On the outbreak of the First World War, the cyclist battalions were employed on coastal defences in the United Kingdom. Their role was

The Ox & Bucks at the Battle of Delville Wood

considered to be so important that, initially, none of them was sent overseas.

Once they were sent abroad, it was in small groups of men, with the divisions possessing individual cyclist companies and composite battalions later formed at corps level. These were rarely committed to action, rather being held back in preparation for the resumption of 'normal' mobile warfare. Cyclists were employed in combat, but in conditions of trench warfare they were generally found to be ineffective. In 1918, however, with the deadlock of the trenches overcome, cyclists once more proved invaluable for reconnaissance.

George Knipe was discharged suffering from pulmonary tuberculosis in September 1918. He and the Army were probably glad to see the back of one another. George's conduct was persistently bad – causing disturbance in the barracks, smashing windows, going absent without leave, displaying insolence on parade. He went home and within weeks he married Edith Weaver. They lived with their family in Rack End, and George continued to work as an agricultural labourer. He died at 57 in June 1953.

Archibald and Henry Knipe's mother Sarah died aged 77 in 1930. His eldest brother John died in 1969 aged 86, and William died in 1952 at 68. Mary married Edward Booth in 1923.

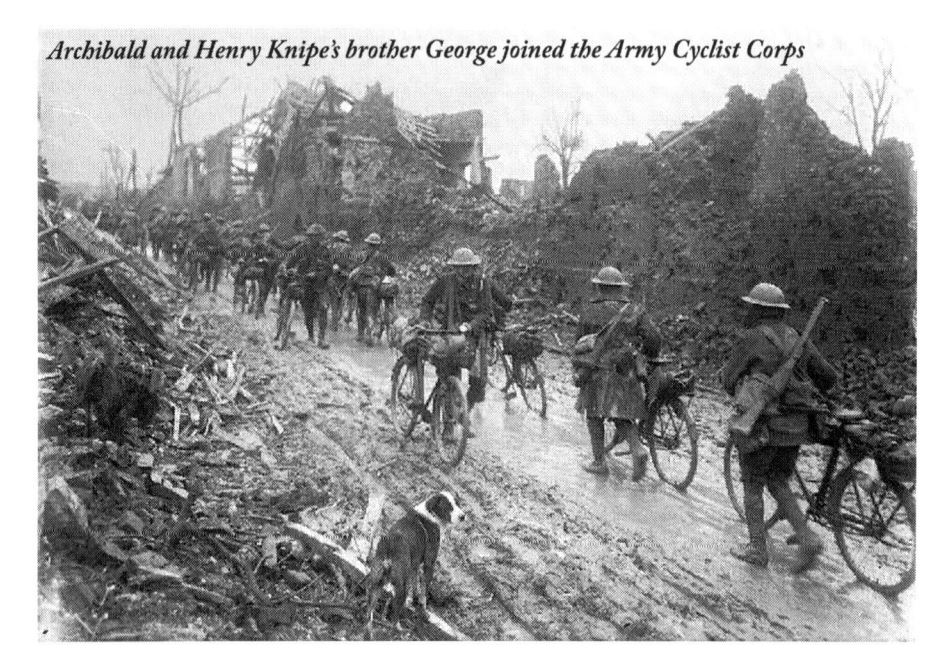

Archibald and Henry Knipe's brother George joined the Army Cyclist Corps

Frederick William Loft

*200832 Corporal, 2nd/4th Battalion,
Oxfordshire & Buckinghamshire Light Infantry*
Standlake

THE NOTION OF Victorian children working in coal mines invokes images of ragamuffins hauling baskets of coal along rails underground. In fact there was a selection of ghastly jobs available above ground too, and one of them fell to the lot of 14 year-old Frederick William Loft of Woolley Colliery near Darton in the West Riding of Yorkshire – an unexpected candidate for a war memorial in rural Oxfordshire.

Woolley Colliery near Darton, with the Loft family home among those in the distance

Nimble-fingered children were employed to screen out stones from the coal

Although Frederick left school to go straight into the dreary job of colliery screens – a noisy, dirty job on the surface where young boys had to sort the stone from the coal – his future was not the worst of the worst. His father, Suffolk-born Frederick Loft, was in the respected position of colliery engine fitter, a skilled mechanic who maintained and overhauled engines and also assembled the various engine parts from blue-prints and specifications. Provided Frederick junior was equipped by nature with the necessary intellect, there was no reason why he shouldn't follow in his father's footsteps. Indeed, at 16 Frederick's brother Albert had already achieved the respectable rank of engine driver, but he died three years later. Concerns about working conditions and safety were expressed regularly by the Yorkshire Miners' Association.

Imagine the courage, therefore, of a boy who announces to his working-class Yorkshireman father that he has found God. At least, it appears that something of the sort happened. For in 1911 we find 24 year-old Frederick in

The Rectory in Standlake: Frederick Loft's home in 1911

The Rectory, Standlake.

the position of 'assistant' to Thomas Lovett, rector of Standlake. Alternatively, as this was the year in which the restoration of the church of St Giles was completed, another theory might place Frederick in the parish on some kind of engineering assignment.

At the end of 1916, British attacks on the Somme front stopped for the

Perhaps Frederick was assisting Reverend Lovett with the refurbishment of St Giles'

The Parish Church, Standlake.

winter. For the rest of the year and into early January 1917, both sides were reduced to surviving the rain, snow, fog, mud, waterlogged trenches, and shell-holes. A thaw set in on 16th February and at dawn on 17th there were dark clouds overhead and a ground mist. The terrain underfoot became soft and slippery before reverting to deep mud. These were the conditions at the start of the Actions of Miramount.

At 4.30 am the German artillery bombarded the front from which the British were to attack, apparently alerted by a deserter. The German bombardment caused many casualties as the British infantry assembled but, in the hope that the German artillery would not be provoked, no retaliatory fire was given. A subsidiary attack on the right flank disappeared into the dark until 9.00 am, when it was reported that the attackers had been repulsed; British casualties and daylight made a resumption of the attack impossible.

Frederick died of his wounds in hospital in Oxford on 6th April 1917. He was 30. Ironically, had Frederick remained at the pit, he might have been exempt from going to the Front. Coal mining was a reserved occupation.

Without a post-war career as confirmation, it seems unlikely we will ever know why Frederick was in Standlake. However, if he was in the area purely to work, his inclusion on the World War I monument in the village is puzzling. Generally a name was listed where the soldier's next of kin lived. And it's not as if Mr and Mrs Loft didn't lay claim to his memory too; the smart stone cross in the churchyard of St Peter's in Woolley which also commemorates Frederick must have stretched their resources considerably.

Frederick's mother Sarah probably never saw the splendid monument to her son. She died in the following year aged 59. His father lived long enough to see the end of World War II, dying aged 90 in 1946.

Frederick Miles
16500 Private, 1st Battalion, Royal Hampshire Regiment
Standlake

WHEN FREDERICK MILES's mother Emma was left a widow at 39 with eight children to support, there was only one thing for it. She must find herself another husband.

Emma, née Coombs, had married Shifford carter Robert Miles in 1867, and the couple had eleven babies at Coldharbour Cottages, eight of whom survived: Ernest, Robert, Herbert Walter, Florence Emma, Alice Maud, Theresa, Frederick, and Alfred. But now Frederick's father was gone so Emma

Coldharbour Cottages at Shifford: gutted by fire in 1974 and never rebuilt

moved her family of six children to Church End, and her widowed mother Sarah Coombs moved in too. But Sarah was ailing, and for Emma going out to work with six children still at home to be looked after was impossible. So in March 1892 Emma presented eight year-old Frederick Miles and his siblings with a step-father in the shape of 56 year-old widower William Johnson. Emma's mother Sarah died in the following year.

Money was short; in 1901 William Johnson was still toiling as an agricultural labourer at 68, and Emma's youngest son Alfred Miles – now the only child still at home – was a farm servant at 13. Ernest was by now married and working as a shepherd on a farm, and living with his family at Brittenden. Robert was boarding with a family in Clewer, Berkshire and working as a labourer. Frederick had been despatched to board with a Johnson relative, and Walter was living with his wife Alice at Church End. Florence was in service to china and glass merchant Walter Cox and his family in Chalfont Road, Oxford, and Alice Maud was in service to brewer's manager William Gillett and his family in Market Square, Witney. Theresa was in service to an elderly widow and her companion in Aston Street in Oxford.

The Johnson relative who took Frederick in was 31 year-old William James Johnson. William James had moved to Simpson in Buckinghamshire (now subsumed into Milton Keynes) and worked as a steam-roller driver. Eighteen year-old Frederick Miles was a road sweeper. This combination of employment suggests that William James and Frederick were working as part of a gang, with Frederick spreading crushed stone onto the road with a broom, and William James steam-rollering it flat to create a compact surface in the process known as macadamisation.

Frederick's step-father William Johnson died in June 1903 at the age of 71, and the youngest Miles boy, Alfred, died five years later aged 21. By 1911 two of Emma's sons were living with her again: Robert and Frederick. Both worked as agricultural labourers.

From the end of the Battles of Ypres and Festubert in May 1915 until the September opening of the Battle of Loos and the French attacks in Champagne,

A road-mending gang like the one Frederick Miles worked in

there was no general change in the situation on the Western Front. It was a period of static warfare, where the army suffered average losses of 300 men a day from sniping and shellfire.

During the first nine days of July 1917, Frederick's battalion, the 1st Battalion, Royal Hampshire Regiment, suffered daily losses in double figures, killed and wounded. On the 9th the battalion doctor went up to the trench to help those who, like Frederick Miles, lay with terrible wounds in the oppressive heat. According to the battalion war diary: 'About 5.15 am our splendid "Doc" (Captain J C Gwynne RAMC) went up to the trench to see what he could do. He spent a long time tending the wounded… No sooner had he finished and straightened himself than a sniper shot him through the head, killing him instantly, and we lost one of the finest and bravest members of the battalion.' It is difficult to imagine the impact of this sight on those injured soldiers who had only minutes before been so grateful for the attentions of such a dedicated man, and upon those who still awaited help.

Frederick Miles died of his wounds on 8th October 1915 aged 32. His mother Emma died in 1923 aged 76.

Cyril F Peart
57356 Private, 3rd Battalion, Royal Worcestershire Regiment
Standlake

THE RAILWAY CAME LATE to Witney, and even then travellers still had to be conveyed to the station from outlying villages. Cyril's father Walter Peart described himself as a coachman/groom – 'not domestic' – on his census return of 1901. The position of the Peart family's entry on the form immediately above that of the Bell Hotel suggests that they may have lived in a cottage adjoining the pub while Walter worked in the commercial coaching trade attached to the inn.

Walter Peart came from Turkdean in Gloucestershire. His first wife Mary

A view showing the cottages and stables once adjacent to the Bell

died giving birth to Cyril's half-brother Tom in September 1896. Two years later, Walter re-married to Annie Florey from Shifford, and Cyril – known in the family as 'Frank' – was born six months later. Perhaps as a reflection of the waning coaching business, enterprising Annie contributed to the household finances during these early child-bearing years. Before the demands of too many babies overwhelmed her, Annie set up as a self-employed linen draper working from home, with an aunt, Anne Florey, to help run the house.

The next child was Laura Jessie in March 1900, then Olive Hilda in March 1902, Charles George in March 1904, and Sidney Herbert in March 1907. In 1911 Cyril's father Walter was working at one of Standlake's four mills, and his half-brother Tom earned his living as an agricultural labourer.

In 1916 at the age of 17, Cyril signed up with the Queen's Own Oxfordshire Hussars. A few months later he was transferred to the Ox & Bucks Light Infantry, and then in 1918 he was attached to the Worcestershire Regiment.

In the spring of 1918 the Germans had realised that their only remaining chance of victory was to defeat the Allies before the overwhelming resources of the United States could be fully deployed. The Spring Offensive was planned by General Ludendorff with the objective of capturing Ypres, and driving the British forces back to the channel ports and out of the war. Estimates of casualties vary as always, but one historian puts the figures for the Spring Offensive at 22,000 British dead, 75,000 prisoners and 63,000 wounded. French casualties were estimated at 80,000 and German at 250,000, including 50–60,000 lightly wounded.

On 24th April 1918 Cyril was shot, the bullet passing straight through his left lung. He was taken to Base Hospital Number 5 at Camiers.

Owing to the large number of casualties, particularly during an offensive, it became necessary to handle the wounded efficiently. A system of general hospitals of varying capacities from 500 to 2,000 patients was established along the main lines of communication on the British front. Hospitals for the care of the wounded on the Ypres-Armentieres-Arras sectors were located along the main lateral line of communication, Calais–Boulogne–Etaples,

Patients at Base Hospital Number 5 were housed in tents like these until 1917

while Le Treport–Abbeville–Amiens–Rouen–Le Havre served for the areas of the Somme battlefield. Specially-equipped ambulance trains assisted by co-ordinated corps of ambulance drivers, among whom were many women of the Voluntary Aid Detachment, made the task of transporting the wounded a highly-perfected operation.

At Camiers, tuberculosis set in and in May Cyril was brought back to the Royal Chest Hospital in London where his condition was deemed inoperable. His raging temperature never dropped back to normal levels, and the medical board approved his discharge on 21st December 1918. He was sent home in January and died in the spring.

On 29th April 1919 Cyril Peart was buried at the church of St Giles in Standlake. He was 20. His mother Annie died aged 67 in Oxford in 1944.

Herbert T R Pickford
2nd Lieutenant,
Oxfordshire & Buckinghamshire Light Infantry
Standlake

PHOTOGRAPHS OF the Pickford family larking around with a motorcar outside the conservatory at Yew Tree Farm in Standlake epitomise our idea of an elegant, self-confident Britain at the beginning of a new century. They bring to mind the world of *Mary Poppins* and *Chitty Chitty Bang Bang*, so soon to disappear forever – if it ever happened at all, which historians question.

The Pickfords lived through the classic, if mythical, 'long Edwardian summer'

Yew Tree Farm, Standlake

As a young man, Herbert Thomas Reade Pickford could afford to look to his future with optimism. He was the elder of two sons of the energetic farmer Thomas Reade Pickford and his wife Annie Watkins.

He was born in Blunsdon near Highworth, Wiltshire in September 1896 but, while Herbert was still an infant, the little family moved to a farm at Coleshill, Berkshire, where younger son Edward William was born. Thomas Pickford was ambitious and, a few years later, he moved his family once more, this time to Standlake where he had spotted the potential of Yew Tree Farm.

The boys were despatched as weekly-boarders to Burford Grammar School. The arrival of a new headmaster in recent years had led to the addition of agricultural studies to the traditional curriculum. A boarding house was established to house pupils during the week, where previously they had been parked with local residents in the town. These developments brought in the sons of local farmers and led to the establishment of a very successful 56-acre farm unit with a Danish Jersey herd, breeding ewes, sows and poultry.

Burford Grammar became a popular destination for the sons of farmers

The Ox & Bucks Light Infantry was deployed in October 1915 to craggy Salonika in Greece where the British Army objective was to assist the Serbs in their fight against Bulgarian aggression. In a letter dated 31st March 1917, Herbert wrote from his bunk there to thank the children of Standlake school for the present they had sent to him. He had only twenty-four days left to live.

In the language of the time, volume 20 of *The Times History of the War* describes the man-made hell into which Herbert Pickford was sent on the night of 24th–25th April 1917: 'When the infantry attacking this particularly difficult sector went over their parapets at 9.45 pm, they had first to clamber down into Jumeaux ravine under a hail of machine-gun bullets, to ford the cascade at the bottom, in places waist-deep, and then to scale the steep slope on the other side with the Bulgarians waiting for them in their trenches along the top.

'In addition to all this, as soon as the first wave of the British went over, the Bulgarian trench mortars and medium artillery started dropping a barrage into

Night-time barrage

the ravine with deadly accuracy. It was like pitching pebbles into a trough, or to use the simile of an officer present, "like standing in a well and having bricks pitched at you".

'To this trench-mortar barrage was added a bombardment by eight-inch howitzers upon our front-line trenches and the ground in front of them. Soaring Very lights [flares fired into the air from a pistol] and two powerful enemy searchlights kept the bare ground under a ghastly illumination. Heavily though we had shelled the Bulgar front line his men had found secure shelter in the ravines close behind, and they were now rushed up to the trenches, where they fought with true Bulgur *sang froid*.'

By 8 pm the British had retreated. Herbert was never seen again. He has no known grave, so his may well have been among the 2,250 bodies buried by the victorious Bulgar defenders.

In 1920 Thomas and Edward Pickford formed a partnership, Pickford & Son, to carry on their business on farms at Standlake and Hardwick. They continued to acquire and develop farmland in the local area. Thomas died in 1949, leaving £5,490 11s 2d. Edward's death was registered in Oxford in 1966.

Tom Shepherd
*13838 Corporal, 7th Battalion,
Oxfordshire & Buckinghamshire Light Infantry*
Standlake

COKETHORPE PARK was the foremost gentleman's residence in the Lower Windrush Valley. Apart from the dozen or so domestic servants living-in, the lives of many local people were bound up with running the house, park, and farm. Tom Shepherd's father Thomas was a farm labourer at Cokethorpe Home Farm. He had married Tom's mother Elizabeth Lacy in 1890 and Elizabeth brought with her to the marriage a daughter named Lizzie Lacy, aged 6. Tom was born in late 1891, and Beatrice, Olive, Belinda Ellen, and Annie Violet followed.

Cokethorpe was occupied for much of the late nineteenth and early

Cokethorpe Park

The Cokethorpe stables: groom Tom Shepherd's workplace

twentieth century by John Cottrell-Dormer. Cottrell-Dormer was born at Bampton, and regularly rode as an amateur jockey. He finished second in the 1892 Grand National on the favourite, *Cloister*, then lost an eye in a ghastly fall at Sandown in 1892.

By 1901, Tom's step-sister Lizzie Lacy was in service with the Butts family in Hampstead. London-born Herbert Butts was a 'managing clerk', and Mrs Butts, née Ellen Woodbridge, was a Ducklington farmer's daughter, suggesting that the placement was perhaps arranged under the auspices of Cokethorpe Park.

In 1908 the Cokethorpe estate was sold to Captain P H G Feilden who lived there from 1911. Feilden was former ADC to the Governor of Queensland, Australia. By this time, the Shepherd family was at Yelford Cottage in Hardwick. Tom's father was still a farm labourer, and Tom himself, now aged 19, was working as a groom. The present college quadrangle at Cokethorpe School was once the domain of horses and ostlers.

Tom's sisters Belinda and Annie were still at home, and his mother Elizabeth was working as an occasional washerwoman, probably to the big house at Cokethorpe when rooms were being used for entertaining. Beatrice was in service to tailor Archibald Valentine and his family in Market Square in Witney, currently occupied by the Steamer Trading Cookshop.

During the first half of October 1916 Tom's regiment, the 7th Battalion, Ox & Bucks LI, was in Salonika. These weeks were spent in training of all kinds, and the whole battalion was inoculated against cholera. According to the regimental war diary of Major C Wheeler DSO, October 17th was quiet and uneventful, 'but at 9 pm the enemy artillery put down a very heavy barrage… All communication with our artillery had been cut by the enemy shells in the first few minutes, so the SOS was sent up. At about 9.45 pm the enemy shelling died down, but at 10 pm opened again. For a quarter of an hour our trenches were heavily bombarded, and our sole remaining wire to the rear was cut, while simultaneously the enemy opened steady rifle and machine-gun fire on our trenches. By 11 pm all firing had ceased, and our officer's patrols went out and searched the ground in front, but found nothing of interest.

'The fact is, that we found fire-control extremely difficult, because of the narrowness of the trenches and the impossibility of keeping touch with the machine-gun company, [who seemed to be] under the impression that until their own officer ordered them to cease they were to blaze away for all they were worth. Except from the noise of the firing, Battalion HQ (only 100 yards away) had little knowledge of what was going on… Casualties 2 men killed and 11 wounded.'

Eight more men were wounded over the next couple of days. Then on October 21st, reported Major Wheeler, the Ox & Bucks endured another bombardment. 'At 1 am the enemy repeated last Tuesday's attack in almost every detail. 5 men were wounded.'

Any of these injured men could have been Tom Shepherd; he died of his wounds on 29th October 1916 aged 24.

Captain P H G Feilden occupied Cokethorpe Park until his death in 1944. He was succeeded by his son Major-General (later Sir) Randle Guy Feilden. In 1957 the house and part of the park were let to Francis Brown, who opened Cokethorpe School. In 1966 the school trustees bought the freehold.

C J Siret
415036 Rifleman, 9th Battalion, London Regiment (Queen Victoria's Rifles)
Standlake

CHARLES JAMES SIRET was one of three children at the Golden Balls Inn in Brighthampton. But the Siret family had taken a circuitous route to arrive there. Charles was born in March 1898 in Calmore on the edge of the New Forest. His father Charles William was the son of a Lambeth carpenter who appears to have had difficulty settling in one place. He married Alice Jane Curtis in 1893, and for the first few years of their marriage the couple moved around Somerset and Hampshire until a development in the Curtis family decided their fate.

For Alice Jane was originally a Cumnor girl whose family had kept the lock at Pinkhill since 1881. When the lock-keeper William Curtis retired in July 1899, Charles and Alice saw an opportunity for a new life. Thames lock-keepers assisted boatmen and bargemen to navigate the change in river level by means of traversing a lock. They charged a toll for each craft, and some supplemented their income by offering refreshment to travellers too.

The Sirets arrived with three small children, Gladys, 4, John, 3, and baby Charles. Nowadays we might shudder at the idea of bringing up young children on an island in a river, but generations of lock-keepers felt no such fear. The Siret children raced around a garden which Thames writer Fred Thacker describes as 'a rambling wilderness of a garden, full of vegetable patches and familiar old-world flowers'. Indeed, in October 1900 *Jackson's Oxford Journal*

Pinkhill Lock

reported that Charles's father had grown a gourd weighing an alleged 100 lb.

After about ten years at Pinkhill Lock, the Sirets were on the move again. The traffic on the upper Thames had been much affected by the opening of the canals, so Charles's father sought out a more definite source of custom in the residents of Brighthampton at the Golden Balls inn. At the age of 13 Charles was still at school, whereas many boys of the same age from poorer

Charles Siret senior (left). Charles junior probably wears the white coat

families in the village were out working by that time. Sixteen year-old Gladys was working as a dressmaker (no point wasting money on educating a girl), and 15 year-old John was assisting in the pub, as was the children's mother Alice.

In 1915 Charles's father enlisted in the Territorials, having served in his youth in the Royal Garrison Artillery. He was posted first to the 4th Ox & Bucks Territorial Force, and then to 258th Company, Royal Defence Corps Territorial Force.

Charles's own regiment, the London Regiment (Queen Victoria's Rifles), was formed on the outbreak of war in August 1914, and volunteers flooded in. The 9th Battalion landed at Le Havre on 4th February 1917. According to *longlongtrail.co.uk*, that summer 'the British finally got what they had wanted since 1914: the opportunity to attack at Ypres and break out of the confines of the salient of trenches around it.

'Often known as the Third Battle of Ypres or Passchendaele, the offensive began with encouraging gains, but terrible summer weather soon bogged it down. By August the offensive was clearly failing in its objectives and had descended into attritional fighting. New techniques by both sides led to agonisingly slow forward movement for the British, at enormous cost in casualties to both sides.' These casualties included Charles James Siret, who was killed in action on 8th September 1917 aged 19.

Nine days later Charles's father was discharged from the Territorial Force as physically unfit owing to chronic rheumatism and bronchitis. He died in the following summer aged 53. Charles's mother Alice retreated with an Army pension of 15 shillings a week to Pinkhill. Perhaps the lock was once more in the hands of a Curtis relative.

In 1924 Charles's sister Gladys married Canadian foundry worker Leonard Brewin in Lambton, Ontario. Also in 1924, John married Violet Comley in 1924, and one hopes that the couple's many children and grandchildren brought poor Alice some joy in her later years.

Harry Sirman

*3011 Private, B Company, 1st/4th Battalion,
Oxfordshire & Buckinghamshire Light Infantry*

Stanton Harcourt

LOSING THE ONLY SON in the family was a particular blow according to the morés of society of the time. And Henry Sirman senior had waited such a long time for his son Harry.

Harry's father had first been married to Mary Clack from Hardwick. The couple had a daughter Mary Ann ('Annie') while still living with Mary's parents in Hardwick, and then moved to Henry's native village of Stanton Harcourt. There they had three more daughters, Rachel, Norah, and Esther.

In March 1885, when little Esther was 6, the girls' mother Mary died. After five years of widowhood, Henry married for a second time. His new wife was former domestic nursemaid Françoise Charlotte Etasse ('Charlotte'), a Frenchwoman and British subject. Eighteen months after the marriage, Harry was born in December 1891. Henry senior was 46.

Fortunately, all of Harry's half-sisters found husbands before war broke out. It is unlikely that four girls from the same family would all have married after the losses of 1914–18. Mary Ann married cowman James John Brucker in March 1902, and her father was obliged to sign the register with a cross. Rachel married Stanton Harcourt cattleman George Belcher in March 1906. Esther married bricklayer's labourer Frederick Watts in June 1907 and moved to her husband's home town of Peterborough. Norah married Stanton Harcourt agricultural labourer William J Burden in December 1910.

When Harry's father was married to his first wife, he worked as a 'machinist' – perhaps operating the new threshing ('thrashing') or binding machinery which was becoming available to farmers. But by 1891 he was a simple agricultural labourer – albeit one with an exotic new wife named Françoise; she seems to have settled upon her middle name 'Charlotte' on the basis, presumably, that it was easier for leaden Anglo-Saxon tongues to manage.

By 1911 just the two men were left at home, with Henry senior, 65, still working on the land and Harry, 19, as an under-carter. It is not clear where Harry's mother Charlotte was; Henry senior still described himself as married, although Charlotte had not featured on the census return since 1891. Perhaps she had to return to France for some reason. If so, one wonders whether she ever saw her son again.

The Battle of Pozières (23rd July–3rd September 1916) took place around the French village of Pozières during the Battle of the Somme. Pozières was an important German defensive position; the fortified village was an outpost to the second defensive trench system.

The infantry was scheduled to attack the German position at 12.30 am on

Machinery for threshing and binding was becoming a more common sight in the fields

A fatigue party heads for the fighting at Pozières

23rd July, with the Australian 1st and 3rd Brigades. The infantry crept into no-man's land close behind the bombardment and, when it lifted, the German trenches were rushed. The battalion war diary reports heavy retaliatory shelling all day. 'In the afternoon,' it reports, 'it became evident that Battalion had suffered heavily, and information was received that Battalion would be relieved.'

Ten officers were killed, wounded, or missing; of the other ranks, 164 were wounded, 16 were missing, and 40 were killed. Harry was among the dead; he was 24.

A pension payment of 18s 7d was made to Harry's father Henry in November 1916. Poor Henry died in March 1919 aged 74, having lost his only son and the companion of his old age. So the final payment of 8s 10d was made to Harry's half-sister Rachel Belcher. No mention is made of Harry's mother Charlotte.

Albert E Smith
J/15293 Able Seaman, HMS Opal
Standlake

ALTHOUGH THIS BOOK is not a military history, the sheer contrast between Albert Edward Smith's unassuming life and the drama of his death is worth noting. Albert's background is a familiar one. He was born in Standlake on 18th December 1895, the son of George Smith and Mary Ann Turner. George was a carter on Batts Farm, Albert's eldest brother Hedley George was a poultryman, and Albert and his other brother William were farm-workers too.

Albert served as an able seaman aboard HMS *Opal*, a Royal Navy destroyer based at Scapa Flow in the Orkneys. Although *Opal* took part in some famous encounters such as the Battle of Jutland, her regular duties consisted of minesweeping, convoy protection and anti-submarine patrols in the North Sea.

On 12th January 1918, *Opal* joined her sister ship *Narborough* and the light cruiser *Boadicea* on a night patrol to hunt for German ships suspected to be laying mines on the Scottish coast. By 5.30 pm, the weather had closed in so much that *Boadicea* ordered *Opal* and *Narborough* back to Scapa Flow while she went on alone.

The only surviving witness to what happened next was Albert's fellow able seaman, William Sissons. His matter-of-fact account contains no trace of self-pity, but at the same time reveals the full horror of his shipmates' last minutes in the freezing sea: 'We turned and headed for harbour. The weather getting worse, a blinding snowstorm and blizzard… We were still in plenty of

River Windrush

water. About 9.30 pm there was a bump and a grating and we realised we were aground. The engines were put into full-speed astern; it was no use, we were jammed. We had a stern sea all the way which was filling the ship up. It was impossible to see the foc's'le head.'

Both *Opal* and *Narborough* had run ashore on the rocks of South Ronaldsay in zero visibility.

South Ronaldsay

Sissons continues: 'On grounding I got back to my gun platform. The crew who were in the foc's'le asleep rushed out, at the same time a sea rushed along the deck and knocked some men over the side, others clambered into the whaler, and as the whaler was being lowered another sea cleared the deck hitting the whaler and breaking the davits.

'I then got around the funnel on to a lifebelt rack. The weather was now much worse, my hands were frozen; as I had a knife I was able to cut the cover of the lifebelt rack and get at the lifebelts. I passed the lifebelts out to some of the men who were sitting on a carly float [emergency raft] between the funnels. I then felt for another lifebelt which was at the bottom, the only one left; at the same time a sea passed over us and it pushed me in the rack.

'When I got out with the only lifebelt, the carly float men were gone. I then put the lifebelt on and jumped up to the angle iron that held the sirens and pulled myself up and got into the funnel. There was already four or five men sitting on the grating inside the funnel. I stood with my back to the sea which was now breaking over the funnel. After being in the funnel for about twenty minutes, things began to get moving. The foremost funnel broke at the deck and fell into the water, then the after-funnel bridge went, leaving the centre funnel I was in. Then the funnel tilted, I jumped out and was left to the mercy of the sea.'

Both wrecks were abandoned and broken up by the sea over the next few weeks taking the bodies of both crews with them, all but the lone survivor William Sissons.

Ninety-five men perished on HMS *Opal* and 93 on *Narborough*. Albert Edward Smith was 22. Albert's mother Mary Ann had died in 1912 aged 43, before the war started. His father George Smith died in 1935 aged 73.

Harry Talbot
*18232 Serjeant, 58th Battery,
35th Brigade, Royal Field Artillery*
Stanton Harcourt

HARDLY ANYONE REMEMBERS that the British fought alongside the Italians in World War I. The matter became something of an embarrassment following the rise of Mussolini's Fascists during the 1920s. At 41, Harry Talbot was one of the older servicemen from the Lower Windrush Valley lost during World War I, and the only one killed in Italy.

When Harry married Lena Batts in Stanton Harcourt in early 1914, like many humble people they had probably never even heard of Franz Ferdinand, the Archduke whose assassination in far-off Sarajevo proved to be the catalyst for world war. Whilst the long Edwardian summer of croquet, motor cars and ragtime may have been reserved for well-off families like the Pickfords of Standlake, strikes on the railways, in the mines and at ports, unrest in Ireland, and Suffragettes smashing shop windows in Oxford Street were probably also outside the day-to-day experience of the villagers of the Lower Windrush Valley.

The Talbots had come to Stanton Harcourt from Sutton Courtenay. Harry's father was Richard Talbot, a threshing machine driver. With his first wife Esther, Richard had seven children. Esther died in 1895, and in 1899 Richard took a second wife, Minnie Webb.

The Italians entered the war on the Allied side, declaring war on Austria in May 1915. Three months later, Harry arrived in France. In the autumn of 1917 the Italians were fighting the Austrians and the Germans at the twelfth and final Battle of the Isonzo – and they were losing badly. British reinforcements were sent for.

On *news.bbc.co.uk*, army chaplain Andrew Martlew describes what happened: 'They came straight out of the trenches of Flanders, from the cold and rain, the mud, and the poison gas. As they travelled down through France, the days got warmer.

'In Italy, they had oranges and figs thrown to them as they marched to reinforce the Italian line. Some were lucky, they moved into trenches that were on warm, dry hills. Others were not so fortunate. The swamps north of Venice meant a return to the familiar mud, with the added joys of mosquitoes and malaria.

'But in the early spring they left the Venetian plain and marched towards the foothills of the Alps which rise, without preamble, straight from sea-level to 3,000 feet (900 metres) and more. They managed the ascent by marching for twenty minutes then stopping for ten, through an achingly long day. And they found a very different world.

'In many places, the pinewoods were still standing as they are now. Cool and shady today, but then still covered with snow and liable to burst into flames during Austrian artillery bombardments. And the trenches are still there too… But they are nothing like the military engineering of Flanders. No complex dugouts with wooden walls and beds for officers. Here the trenches were hewn and blasted out of solid rock.'

The front was comparatively quiet until the Austrians attacked in force from Grappa to Canove in the Battle of Asiago (15th–16th June 1918). The Allied line was penetrated to a depth of about 1,000 metres on 15th June, and Harry Talbot was among heavy losses suffered that day, killed in action at the age of 41.

Harry's father Richard Talbot did not live to see his son's death. He died aged 62 in 1917. Minnie lived long enough to see war start all over again, dying in 1940 aged 68.

Above: Men of the Royal Field Artillery requisition state-of-the-art transport in Asiago
Below: A rapidly-changing Stanton Harcourt that Harry Talbot did not live to see

141

John James Tidmarsh
10690 Private, 5th Battalion,
Oxfordshire & Buckinghamshire Light Infantry
Northmoor

IF EVER THE FRONT COVER of this book were said to portray any one of the servicemen commemorated within its pages, it would be John James Tidmarsh. John was baptised on Christmas Day in 1897 at Wootton by Woodstock, the son of cattleman John Tidmarsh and his wife Ellen, formerly Smith.

John senior had been a prize-winning ploughboy in his youth. *Jackson's Oxford Journal* reports that, at the annual Woodstock Agricultural and Horticultural Show in 1887, he received the award made 'to the ploughboy, under 18 years of age, who shall plough his half an acre of land with three horses, according to the regulations'.

John James had an older sister and brother, Elsie and Albert, and then after the family moved to Ellen's home parish of Glympton, a third boy, Wilfred, was born. In 1911 the family was in Chapel Lane in Northmoor, and the number of children had risen to nine. John senior was working as a carter on a farm, John James's older brother Albert, 15, as a cattleman, and at 13 John James himself was working with horses.

Those who worked with animals were considered a cut above other farm servants. They were generally hired by the year, rather than on a casual basis, and earned higher wages than the labourers. Better pay, of course, served as an inducement to keep children out of school, which is where John should really

Sleek carthorses like these at Watkins Farm were taken to a new life with the Army

have been at 13. But with Wilfred, Mabel, Gladys, and Frederick in school, and Ruby, 2, and baby Dorothy at home, every penny was needed.

On the 1st August 1915 the 5th Battalion, Ox & Bucks was in the neighbourhood of Ypres, holding trenches near the Menin Road. Captain and Adjutant B C T Paget recorded in his diary:

'*August 5th*

'The enemy replied to our artillery bombardment this morning with heavy

Millions of horses, mules, and donkeys died in terrible conditions during the war

field-gun fire and some 5.9s [German field guns]. His mortars were also active, and ours replied. We put 5 mortar bombs into the enemy's redoubt opposite Railway Wood, as a working party was seen there. The situation to-day was altogether more lively than usual. The enemy was trench-mortaring and firing "whizz-bangs" all day. The latter from field-guns caused 95 per cent of our casualties.

'We ourselves replied with trench mortars and catapult bombs. The enemy's aerial-torpedo mortar was located, and one of our 9.2-inch howitzers fired at it, the first shot, it is believed, being a direct hit. I sincerely hope so, as its projectile is very trying to the nerves. Casualties – 2 men killed, and 5 wounded.'

Among the five wounded was John James Tidmarsh.

In spite of unimaginably trying circumstances, impeccable British civilities were maintained. Paget's diary continues: 'Major Webb received the following note from Captain G Willoughby, 9th Rifle Brigade, commanding the company on our right: "May I take the opportunity which the present quiet offers of thanking you and all your battalion for their unceasing kindness to us during the last few days? Wounded men, stretcher-bearers, and everyone who came in contact with your officers or men, all say how very good your battalion were in rendering them assistance in every conceivable way.

'"As officer in charge of the Company on your immediate right, the Company and I wish especially to express our gratitude to you, and at the same time the hope that we may give the Boche a licking in the near future, in company with your battalion."'

John died of his wounds on 27th September 1915 aged 17. He was the youngest soldier recorded on the war memorials of the Lower Windrush Valley.

After the war John James's mother Ellen lived in Drayton St Leonard near Wallingford. She died aged 61 in 1930.

Edwin Trinder

*203347 Private, 2nd/1st Battalion,
Oxfordshire & Buckinghamshire Light Infantry*
Stanton Harcourt

THE NAME 'YPRES' conjures up for the British images of all the worst aspects of trench warfare on the Western Front. Blasted tree stumps in a landscape of mud, flooded trenches, relentless bombardment, brave young men being driven to insanity – such were the last impressions on this Earth experienced by blameless 19 year-old Edwin Trinder from Stanton Harcourt.

Edwin Akers Trinder was born in 1898, the son of shepherd George Trinder and his wife Elizabeth Akers from Brize Norton, a relative of Charles Akers at the Harcourt Arms who also hailed from Brize Norton. Edwin had seven brothers and sisters: Thomas, William, Jessie, Lizzie, Frederick, Annie, and Albert. Edwin fitted in before Albert.

Edwin was still only 13 at the time of the latest available census return, so no clue is given as to what trade he might have followed had international events not overtaken him. His parents took advantage of their connection with the Akers family to place his older brothers Thomas and William as baker's assistants at John Akers' grocer's shop in the main street. And another brother, Frederick, moved in with his uncle Richard Trinder and worked as a jobbing gardener.

The Third Battle of Ypres took place from July to November 1917 for control of the ridges south and east of the Belgian city of Ypres in Western Flanders. On 22nd August 1917 Edwin Trinder's battalion, the 2nd/1st Ox &

STANTON HARCOURT MANOR AND CHURCH, OXON

Bucks, was sent into the attack. At 4.45 am the artillery put down a barrage and the infantry advanced, disregarding the strongposts and pressing forward as closely as possible to the barrage in accordance with the orders they had

A sniper's hide-out disguised as a blasted tree stump

received. The 'moppers-up', in attempting to follow, suffered heavy casualties from machine-gun and rifle fire, as the garrisons of the enemy posts put up stubborn resistance from behind their concrete walls.

The 2nd/1st Ox & Bucks advanced on the point known as 'Kansas Cross', but the supporting companies suffered many casualties when capturing Aisne and Somme Farms. Aisne Farm was retaken by the Germans almost at once. Enemy snipers were much in evidence throughout the day. Any movement that might suggest a runner with information for HQ attracted their special attention; even stretcher-bearers and the wounded crawling painfully back were not spared.

During World War I, the German army earned a reputation for the deadliness and efficiency of its snipers. At first the French and British believed such hits to be coincidental, until the German rifles with telescopic sights were discovered. At the start of the war German industry was way ahead in terms of the quality of the lenses it could manufacture.

The marksmen were usually specially trained, and they rarely worked from their own trenches. The main strategy was to creep out at dawn into no-man's land and remain there all day. Wearing camouflaged clothing and using the cover of, say, a fake tree, they waited for a British soldier to pop his head above the parapet. A common trick was to send up a kite with English wording on it. Anyone who raised his head to read it was shot.

During the course of 22nd–23rd August 1917 and in the subsequent fierce German counter-attack the 61st Division lost 914 men. Edwin Trinder was among those killed on the first day. He was 19.

Having already lost her husband earlier that year, and then Edwin's brother Thomas at the end of April, Edwin's mother Elizabeth received the news that she had lost Edwin too. Perhaps mercifully, she did not survive too long afterwards. She died in 1921 aged 60. In 1920 Jessie Trinder married groundsman Albert Foster from Coventry.

147

Thomas Trinder
*CH/1819(S) Private, 1st RM Battalion,
Chatham Division, Royal Marine Light Infantry*
Stanton Harcourt

CHILDREN GROWING UP without fathers is nothing new. Stanton-born Thomas Trinder left four small sons when he died in northern France, one a mere babe-in-arms. Thomas himself was born in 1887, the son of shepherd George Trinder and his wife Elizabeth Akers from Brize Norton. He had seven brothers and sisters: William, Jessie, Lizzie, Frederick, Annie, Edwin, and Albert.

At first the family lived in Black Ditch, but by 1901 they had moved to the main street. This meant that George and Elizabeth could keep an eye on their two eldest boys because, at 14 and 12, Thomas and William were living at the baker's and grocer's shop with proprietor John Akers – presumably a relative of Elizabeth's. Both boys were working as baker's assistants.

In 1910 Thomas married Charlotte Ware from Stoke Poges in Buckinghamshire and the young couple lived in the Ware household in Wexham Street. Thomas worked as a baker journeyman, a term which makes him sound like some sort of travelling salesman who turns up on the doorstop offering a selection of buns. In fact, the term probably referred to the fact that Thomas was paid by the day for his work (from the French *journée* = day). Thomas and Charlotte had five sons: Thomas, who died as an infant in 1911, George in 1912, Reginald in 1913, Philip in 1914, and Robert in 1916.

Thomas commenced service with the Royal Marines on 11th December

At 14 Thomas Trinder worked as a baker's assistant at Akers' shop

1915. The Battle of Gavrelle on 28th–29th April 1917 was part of the campaign around Arras in northern France. The night before the battle, men from Thomas's battalion were sent to reconnoitre the major defensive position north of the village which they were scheduled to attack the following day. They found to their dismay that the extensive and hefty barbed-wire fencing

British troops at Gavrelle

protecting the position was still intact. This proved to be a major contributing factor to the subsequent very high losses.

At 4.25 am on the 28th the attack started. The 1st Battalion, Royal Marine Light Infantry advanced headlong into a strong point north of the village where the German trench system crossed the railway line. Although some men managed to fight their way through the barbed wire, the flanking units never made contact with them. The battalion was effectively wiped out.

The only form of news was from the few wounded who managed to get back to their own lines, and they said that the first objective had been taken. More evidence comes from the discovery of bodies after the war. Much of the battalion appears to have become trapped the wrong side of intact barbed wire, and conducted a desperate fire fight from there.

It seems that a portion of the first objective was taken, but not in strength. Under orders to continue regardless of what was happening to the sides, some pockets of men got further. The disposition of bodies found after the war suggests that many were killed just behind the German front line; some bodies were found in the area of the first objective and a scattering in the second.

The Battle of Gavrelle saw the highest number of Royal Marine casualties ever sustained in a single day in the history of the corps, with 846 recorded as killed, missing, or wounded. Virtually all the casualties were killed in action but were not identified at the time of burial.

Among them was Thomas Trinder, aged 29. His boys were 5, 4, 3, and an infant under one year. His mother Elizabeth had just lost her husband, Thomas's father George, who died earlier that same year aged 56. Thomas's younger brother Edwin was killed in action four months later (see page 145).

Walter Victor Trinder
30056 Private, 2nd Battalion, Royal Warwickshire Regiment
Stanton Harcourt

THE FAMILIES OF the Lower Windrush Valley were perfectly open to the idea of moving away to improve the life chances of their offspring. Walter Trinder's parents took their children off to Birmingham to seek better opportunities than those which an agricultural life could offer.

Walter's father Henry Trinder, an agricultural labourer, was born in Freeland in 1844. His mother Emily Ayres was born a Stanton girl in 1846. She was Henry's second wife; his first, Ann Calcutt, and her infant daughter, also Ann, had died in 1872. Henry and Emily married in 1877 and quickly had two girls: Edith in 1878, and Lizzie Eva in 1879. At a time when every family wanted a son, the arrival of Walter Victor in 1887, eight years after the birth of their last surviving child, must have seemed something of a gift.

By 1901 the Trinder family had left Sutton for Birmingham to investigate the job opportunities offered by its bustling economy. They lived in Temple Row, now a modern shopping centre, and Henry worked as a caretaker and window cleaner. Only young Walter was living with his parents at this stage. Edith is nowhere to be seen; perhaps she married. Lizzie was in service to three dressmakers in Wretham Road in Handsworth.

By 1911 the Trinders had moved to Farm Street, and sister Lizzie, 31, was back home and involved in dying, cleaning and ironing – perhaps utilising in a laundry or a clothing factory the experience she had gained with the dressmakers. At 23, Walter was a 'shaper and turner' for an electrical engineer.

Farm Street, Birmingham

The Second Battle of Arras was a British offensive on the Western Front. From 9th April to 16th May 1917, British troops attacked German defences near the French city of Arras. The fighting over 3rd–4th May became known as the Third Battle of the Scarpe.

The 2nd Battalion Royal, Warwickshire Regiment participated in the flanking operation at Bullecourt. In the late spring of 1917, the Allies were in crisis. Revolution had erupted in Russia and the French army was on the verge of mutiny. Meanwhile, Germany was winning the war in the air and her U-boats menaced the channel. Despite General 'Thruster' Gough's first assault on the fortress village of Bullecourt using the new wonder-weapon the tank and the Anzacs, the action ended in disaster.

On 3rd May Gough launched a second attack on Bullecourt which dominated the British action on the Western Front for two weeks. The excessive brutality and the ferocity of the hand-to-hand fighting earned Bullecourt the name the 'Blood Tub'. The 3rd May became one of the costliest days of the war in terms of British Empire deaths in one day.

At 4 am on 4th May, as the 2nd Royal Warwickshires formed up ready to advance, a heavy German bombardment hit. The survivors fought their way to an old German trench on the outskirts of the village of Bullecourt, but they were unable to occupy it because it was full to the brim with British and German dead. German sniper fire from the houses in the village also persuaded them of the wisdom of retreat.

In the late afternoon the Warwickshires were ordered forward again. They were greeted by intense machine-gun and small-arms fire from enemy strongpoints in and around Bullecourt, forcing the few survivors to make another hasty retreat. The fighting continued for several more days, but without Walter Victor Trinder. He was killed on 4th May 1917 aged 30.

Having failed to make any significant advances, the attack was called off after incurring heavy casualties. The battle was a disaster for the British Army which suffered nearly 6,000 men killed for little material gain. Walter's father Henry was back in Stanton Harcourt when he died in 1926 aged 83. Walter's mother Emily died in 1929 aged 81.

Bullecourt in ruins

G E Tuckey

S4/217924 Private, 158th Company,
Royal Army Service Corps
Standlake

WAR IS NOT ALL shooting and bombing, and the British Army was quick to exploit any useful skills that men could bring with them from civilian life and put towards the general effort. The fact that George Edwin Tuckey of Standlake was born into a family of bakers did not go unnoticed by the Army Service Corps.

George's father, master baker William Tuckey, married Essex-girl Elizabeth Perry in June 1875, and before George even appeared in October 1882 the couple had already produced three sons, William, John, and Herbert Henry, as well as two after George, Lewis and Percival. Such a wealth of sons did not bode well for George's chances of taking over the family business. It seems no coincidence, either, that the head of the household next door in the main village street was George Blunker, a journeyman bread and biscuit maker. Standlake was blessed for a while with a surfeit of bakers. All six boys assisted in the bakery after leaving school except Percival, who became a postman.

Hardly surprising, then, that by the time George married carpenter and wheelwright's daughter Ellen Jane Long in July 1910, he had left the baking business behind and was making a living as a gardener. The couple had a daughter, Gwendoline Kate, in July 1912.

George was called up on the 19th October 1916. He enlisted in the Army Service Corps, with his occupation listed firmly as 'baker'. The British Army

High Street, Standlake

in France had little need for gardeners. He embarked on the SS *Donegal* from Southampton on 16th April 1917, landing in Le Havre the following day. He came home on leave for the first two weeks of February 1918.

George may have been on duty at the 18th Casualty Clearing Station at Doullens in the Somme department, France when he died there on 1st April

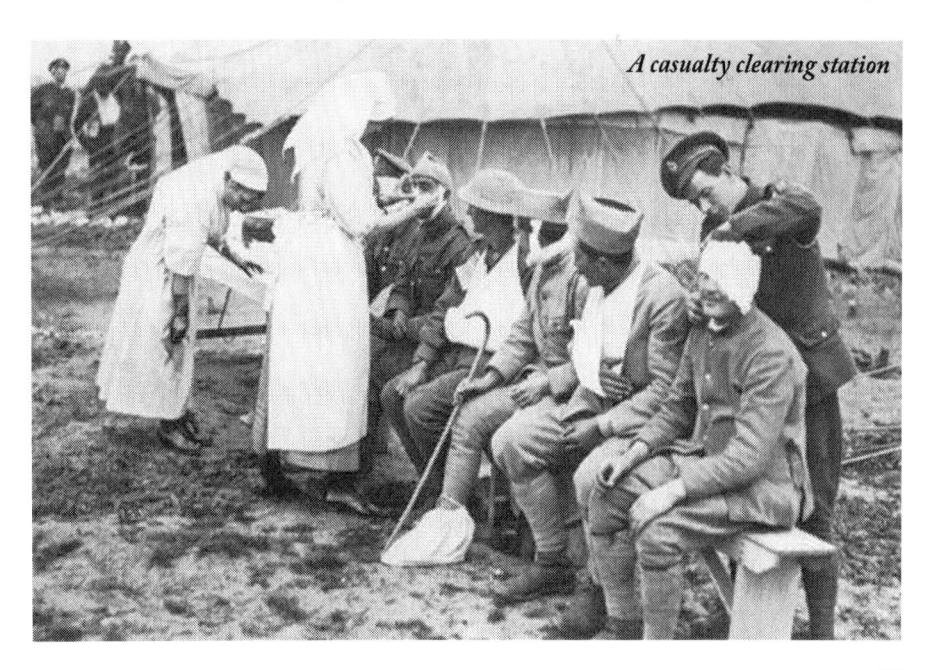

A casualty clearing station

1919. According to *longlongtrail.co.uk*: 'The Casualty Clearing Station [CCS] was part of the casualty evacuation chain, further back from the front line than the Aid Posts and Field Ambulances. It was manned by troops of the Royal Army Medical Corps, with attached Royal Engineers and men of the Army Service Corps. The job of the CCS was to treat a man sufficiently for his return to duty or, in most cases, to enable him to be evacuated to a Base Hospital. It was not a place for a long-term stay.

'CCSs were generally located on or near railway lines, to facilitate movement of casualties from the battlefield and on to the hospitals. Although they were quite large, CCSs moved quite frequently, especially in the wake of the great German attacks in the spring of 1918 and the victorious Allied advance in the summer and autumn of that year.' The 18th had started in Lapugnoy in France, then moved to Lillers, and Arques, then to Malassises in Belgium, and then back to the Pas de Calais in Ypres and finally Doullens.

The cause of George Tuckey's death given by the officer in charge was 'syncope and mitral disease of heart, contracted on active service'. He was 36.

George's brother Herbert had also signed up with the Army Service Corps in 1916 and deployed his baking skills for King and Country. Indeed, Herbert was discharged suffering from what was called 'baker's pneumonia' in 1918. At the age of 38, years of breathing in flour dust had caused him to experience coughing, shortness of breath, wheezing, and chest tightness during an attack.

In 1931 George and Ellen's daughter Gwendoline married Hedley John Smith, son of a Brighthampton farm labourer. They had a daughter called Mavis – George's granddaughter – born in 1938. Unsurprisingly, George's brother Herbert did not make old bones. He died in 1936 aged 55. George's widow Ellen died in 1965 aged 85.

Ernest Walker
*7442 Company Serjeant Major, 2nd Battalion,
Oxfordshire & Buckinghamshire Light Infantry*
Northmoor

WE SOMETIMES IMAGINE that the 'blended' family is a modern phenomenon. Not so. Cottages spilling over with multitudes of children were the result of just as many – perhaps more – single parents re-marrying as do today, though usually as a result of death, not divorce. Ernest Walker grew up in just such a family at Pinnocks Farm.

His mother Sarah, formerly Moss, died aged 36 in 1888 when Ernest was just a toddler. His father George Walker, a simple carter, was left with six children to support financially and somehow to arrange care for. Meanwhile in Stanton Harcourt Selina Anne Batts ('Annie', née Clack) found herself in a similar position to George. Her first husband Richard Batts died in the same year as George's wife Sarah, leaving Annie with four children. After two years of widowhood, George and Annie married, and in 1890 Annie brought her own four children to a household already over-run by six of George's own at Pinnocks Farm where George worked as a labourer.

There is no reason to suppose that George and Annie Walker were any less happy than any other couple, but these second marriages were often based as much on pragmatism as on romance. It was extremely difficult for any lone parent, male or female, to work and care for a young family at the same time. An amalgamation of two widowed parents and their ten orphaned children into one new family unit suited the entire community.

Above: Elsie Foster (left) and her family at The Patch, Northmoor. Below: Guillemont station

158

After ten years, five of the children had moved on, so George and Annie down-sized to a cottage near the church of St Denys. Now aged 47, George supported his reduced family by working as a carter, and 15-year-old Ernest appears to be destined to follow in his father's trade. He was working as a teamster – a driver of a team of horses used for haulage. But then things changed.

By 1911 Ernest had joined up with the Ox & Bucks and risen to Lance Serjeant at the age of 25. And his base at Cowley Barracks seems to be from where he formed an attachment to his future wife. Elsie Mary Foster was a Northmoor girl all right; she grew up at The Patch. But in 1911 she, too, was in Oxford, in service with the family of a retired chemist. Ernest and Elsie married in March 1916.

By the time Ernest's battalion arrived in France in August 1914 he had been promoted company serjeant major. As part of the campaign on the Somme, on 28th July 1916 the 2nd Ox & Bucks moved to front-line trenches near Waterlot Farm (actually a sugar refinery). On the 29th July the 5th Infantry Brigade issued orders for the attack on Guillemont. The battalion war diary explains:

'On the 30th July zero hour was 4.45 am, and the attack commenced in accordance with the timetable. At 6 am the Officer Commanding the regiment sent the following message to Brigade HQ: "Attack on station, at first held up by line of bombing posts, is now getting forward, but I cannot yet tell whether it has reached objective. Heavy casualties."

'…The farthest point reached by the 5th Brigade was Guillemont Station, which officers and men of B and C Companies of the regiment are known to have entered, although none returned…

'Casualties 12 Officers & 205 Other Ranks.'

Ernest Walker was killed in action on 30th July 1916 at the age of 31.

Ernest's widow Elsie remarried to Arnold Smith in 1924.

Percy Walker
14020 Private, 7th Battalion, Wiltshire Regiment
Stanton Harcourt

EVERY ONE OF Percy Walker's siblings went into service except Percy himself. He was born in Sutton in 1892, the son of cowman William Walker and his wife Esther. Percy was the last-but-one of six children, the others being Sarah, Ellen, Ernest, Fanny, and Bessie.

Sarah worked in Cowley for the family of a college steward. Ellen served as a parlour maid at the splendidly Gothic Chesham Bois Place, home of the Cave-Browne family in Buckinghamshire. Ernest first went into service in 1901 as

'Sutton: all that was familiar in an English hamlet…

a boot-room man in Bradfield near Reading, but by 1911 he was married and working as a shop porter for a leather goods merchant in Reading itself.

The two youngest girls stayed within the village. At 14 Fanny was in service to farmer Joseph Walker and his family in Black Ditch where she worked alongside little Alice Allen, aged just 12. Alice was the sister of Frederick Allen (see page 16). Fanny married Leicestershire coal miner William Ayres in 1911, and Bessie worked as a general domestic servant to the family of farmer John Bury. Of all the Walkers' six children, only Percy was left at home at the bottom of Sutton Lane in 1911, aged 19, and working as farm labourer. He was engaged to Eva Burden, whose father Mark had once worked as a shoemaker, but now supported his family as a market gardener.

The Salonika Campaign began on 5th October 1915. The Allies hoped to deter Bulgaria from joining Germany and Austria-Hungary, but only days later Bulgaria declared war on Serbia. Attempts by the Anglo-French force to support the Serbian army ended in failure and by 14th December the troops were back on Greek territory and retreating towards Salonika.

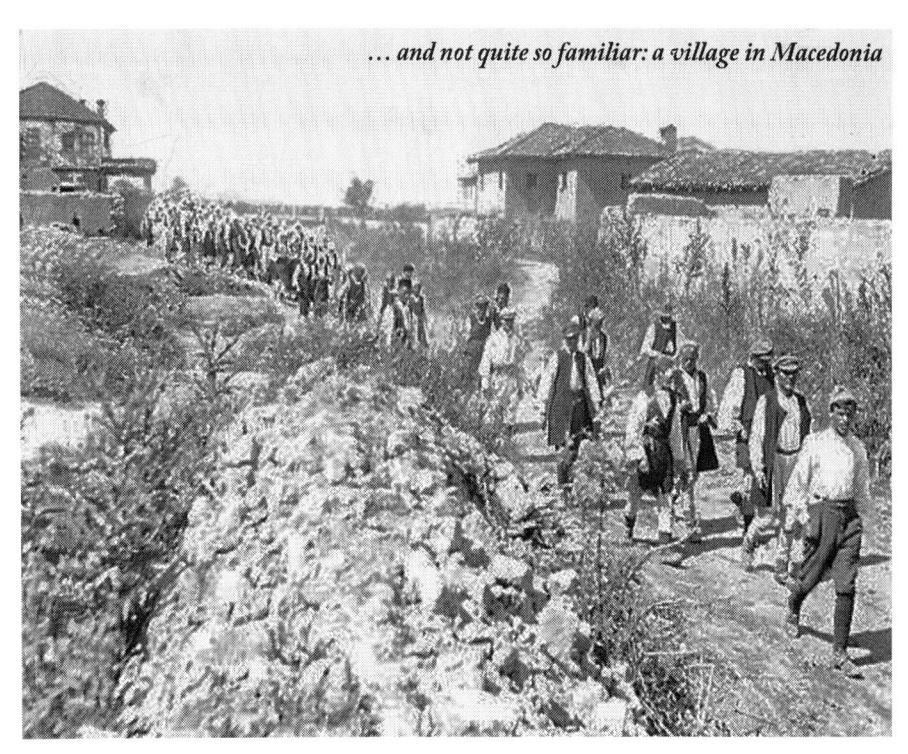

... and not quite so familiar: a village in Macedonia

The Allied army lacked sufficient manpower, ammunition, equipment and supplies to fight a sustained campaign along a 250-mile front against Bulgarian forces and their allies numbering almost 500,000 men. Accommodation for the front-line soldier usually comprised little more than a bivouac tent or dugout. Much effort was expended on improving the local road network and in constructing light railways. Even so, many parts of the front could only be reached by pack mules.

Allied offensives led by French and Serbian troops were launched during late 1916 and the spring of 1917. As part of these operations the British Salonika Force fought the First Battle of Doiran (24th April – 9th May 1917). Author Alan Palmer gives an account in *The Gardeners of Salonika* (Andre Deutsch, 1965): 'As the Wiltshires and the Devons crouched in their trenches, Bulgarian howitzers and a battery of German naval guns pounded the boulders around them. There was a lull in the barrage in the early evening, and from the lakeside a waiting officer heard a familiar sound – the croak of hundreds of frogs, adding a touch of Aristophanic mockery to the irony of war. It was no more than a brief respite. Soon the shells were lobbing down once more; and the gullies became caverns of dead and wounded even before the hour of advance.

'At 9.45 pm, with the relentless barrage unabated, they pressed forward, down to the bottom of the smoke-filled Jumeaux Ravine and across a swift-flowing stream. And when they emerged from the hell of the ravine, two powerful searchlights threw their beams across the open ground, exposing the attackers to a withering cross-fire; few reached the Bulgarian trenches.'

Between 24th April and 9th May, the British Salonika Force suffered more than 5,000 casualties, killed and wounded. One of the missing after the first day was Percy Walker. In fact he had been killed in action on 24th April 1917 aged 26. This failure by the Allies to break Bulgarian resistance resulted in stalemate along the Salonika Front.

Percy's mother Esther died aged 60 in 1915. His father William died in 1944 aged 94. Eva Burden never married. She died in the Wantage area in 1980.

Victor Cecil Walker
67052 Private, Royal Buckinghamshire Hussars
Northmoor

WHEN VICTOR CECIL WALKER was born in the family's cottage in Chapel Lane, Northmoor in December 1899, his father George Walker was, like so many others, working as a carter on a farm. However, this was not the George Walker who lived at Pinnocks Farm with his second wife Annie. Within a few years of Victor's birth, George and his wife Harriett Annie Willson from Watford were running the Red Lion inn.

Untangling the intricacies of the Walker tribe of Northmoor is not the

The Red Lion, Northmoor: Victor Cecil Walker is pictured second from the right

163

business of this book. But the family does serve as an example of how babies received their names. Basically, Christian names identified which branch of a family an individual belonged to. Therefore, a father called Henry Smith would name his first son Henry Smith, his second Robert after his own father. Henry and Robert would each name their two eldest sons Henry and Robert, or Robert and Henry – and so on. There could be multiple Henry and Robert Smiths within one village, all of a similar age. The formula varied, with the names from the mothers' families appearing too. Much corroboration by means of other details – mother's maiden name, wife's name – is required to pin down a particular Smith.

The Red Lion had been in the hands of the Walker clan in the 1880s before it passed to the Hutts, who also held Newbridge Mill and Ferryman's Farm. When Victor Cecil was a boy, the pub was back in the hands of his hard-working father George Walker, who also described himself as a road contractor's labourer, perhaps working for his own uncle, road contractor William Walker.

The Red Lion, like so many English village pubs, originated as a 'church house', that is, a building erected by the ecclesiastical authorities on church land and specifically devoted to the celebration of village festivals. Formerly, these revelries took place in the churchyard itself, but the Pagan derivation of some of this jollity, and its seemingly irreverent nature, persuaded anxious religious authorities to shift the focus of potentially profane behaviour away from sacred ground and into a designated and controllable location. The village pub was born.

While Harriett had her hands full with the pub and seven children, George was a parish councillor too. Throughout the nineteenth century an alliance of landowners and tenant farmers held the reins of power. Non-elected parish vestries and *ad hoc* bodies dealing with sanitation and education contributed to a far from democratic situation. The Local Government Act of 1888 transferred the levying of rates, the maintenance of roads, and of poor relief to county councils elected by ratepayers.

But it was the Local Government Act of 1894 that gave energetic men like

The Walker family at the Red Lion: Victor Cecil is on the left in the back row

The Radcliffe Infirmary in Oxford: several of our servicemen died here

George Walker an opportunity to shape their own communities. It transferred the civil functions of parish vestries to specially-created parish councils, for which someone like Victor's father was now allowed to stand.

So, with every chance of involvement in one of the Walker businesses in due course, and possibly even in local government, literacy would have been an important accomplishment for Victor. His firm and confident – perhaps even flamboyant – handwriting on his enlistment papers confirms this.

Victor would not have known when he enlisted that his military career would be any less heroic than anyone else's. Aged 18 and working as a footman, he signed up on 4th January 1918 and he was posted to 3rd Battalion, Ox & Bucks LI on 12th. Then on 29th March a telegram announced his transfer to the Royal Buckinghamshire Hussars.

By February he was in a military hospital in Dover with suspected tuberculosis, and in July he was discharged. Victor's condition was adjudged to have pre-dated his enlistment, so it seems possible his parents were going to lose him anyway. He died in hospital in Oxford later in 1918. He was 19.

Charles Weston
24452 Private, 10th Battalion,
Princess Charlotte of Wales's (Royal Berkshire) Regiment
Northmoor

AT 48, CHARLES WESTON was one of the oldest volunteers from the Lower Windrush Valley. Was it a rush of patriotism that prompted him to enlist when he didn't need to? Or perhaps a change in his home circumstances made the army seem a reasonable option.

The Military Service Bill, introduced in January 1916, provided for the conscription of single men aged from 18 to 41. So, when Charles travelled to Stow-on-the-Wold to enlist in the 10th Battalion, Princess Charlotte of Wales's (Royal Berkshire) Regiment, he must have been a volunteer; his age was several years higher than the upper limit of 41 as required by the Bill.

Charles was the son of widower and carter William Weston of Chimney. William had been born in Lyford and had married Charles's mother Eleanor New from Stanton in Wiltshire in 1865. Eleanor died in 1898 having given birth to two sons and two daughters: Henry Charles ('Charles'), Thomas, who died aged 7, Mary Ann, and Edith.

By April 1911 Charles's father William was so frail that he required a boarder in the household to sign the census return; later that year he died aged 72. It may be that, with William's death, the family lost a tied cottage. A married man with children who managed farm animals was often provided with accommodation as part of his pay package. Unmarried workers would be boarded with these families around the farm. The Weston home was certainly

Above: Chimney Farm Cottages. Below: Ration boxes at Rouen station

big enough put up three boarders in 1911, a farm-hand, a cowman, and the farm foreman. These last three were all, like Charles, unmarried men without children, so they would not qualify for accommodation as part of their wages.

Although the army in France and Flanders was able to use some existing railways, steam engines, and tracked vehicles for haulage, the immense effort of building and maintaining the huge network of roads, railways, canals, buildings, camps, stores, dumps, telegraph, and telephone systems required for modern warfare relied at first on horse, mule and human. In August 1914 there was no formed body of troops specifically designed for these tasks.

Because of this desperate need for infrastructure at the front, Charles's battalion was formed in 1916 and transferred to the Labour Corps. Units often worked within range of enemy guns, sometimes for lengthy periods, requiring nerves of steel. It is a fallacy that conscientious objectors were deployed in the Labour Corps.

Charles enlisted at Stow-on-the Wold and was posted to the 10th (Labour) Battalion, Princess Charlotte of Wales's (Royal Berkshire) Regiment. Based at Cambridge Barracks in Portsmouth, the 10th Battalion was formed of men who were deemed unsuitable for front-line duties. After October 1915 large numbers of conscripts began arriving and those classified as suitable for Labour Service were initially allocated to Headquarters Works Companies, but these were then formed into the 10th Battalion.

On the 7th May 1916 the 10th were mobilised, but were then delayed by an outbreak of influenza. Finally they embarked for France on the night of the 18th–19th June. They went to Number 3 Labour Camp at Rouen where they were employed loading and unloading supplies from trains.

Charles died on 3rd January 1917, less than six months after arriving in France. He was 50 years old. The cause of Charles's death is unclear, but he was buried in St Sever Cemetery Extension in Rouen which was in the neighbourhood of several hospitals: eight general, five stationary, one British Red Cross, one labour hospital, and Number 2 Convalescent Depot.

Also by Julie Ann Godson

THE WATER GYPSY
How a Thames fishergirl became a viscountess

AT DUSK on a snowy evening in 1766 a tired young couple made out the welcoming lights burning in the windows of creaky old Shellingford Manor in the Vale of the White Horse, the house that was to be their home. He was Viscount Ashbrook, she was Betty Ridge, daughter of a humble Thames fisherman. Earlier that day they had been married in a little village church, and now Betty—a real-life Cinderella—was embarking on a new life in the alien world of the aristocracy.

SCANDAL IN HIGH SOCIETY OXFORDSHIRE
Twenty tales of toffs in trouble

SECRET LOVE AFFAIRS, murder, blackmail, poisoning and extortion: most of us enjoy a good scandal. And it's even more fun when it involves our so-called 'betters'. This book tells twenty tales of Oxfordshire toffs in trouble, from the Tudor period right up to the modern age. Few readers will fail to be impressed by the sheer variety of ways in which the upper classes of the county have contrived over the centuries to behave badly—and often to get away with it.

NORTHMOOR THROUGH THE YEARS

A FASCINATING collection of photographs, maps, documents and newspaper cuttings charting the history of a village by the river Thames in Oxfordshire and the changing lives of its residents.

MEMORIES OF THE VALE

FIRST PUBLISHED in 1866, this account of rural life in the Vale of the White Horse before the railway came was written by Stanford in the Vale curate Rev Lewin G. Maine. This new edition, edited by Julie Ann Godson, contains many names and occupations useful to family history researchers.

THE SCOURING OF THE WHITE HORSE

FIRST PUBLISHED in 1859, this enchanting novel is author Thomas Hughes' way of recording the very last "Pastime", the festival accompanying the 1857 ceremony of Scouring the Uffington White Horse. As well as giving a full account of the history and sports of the Pastime, this new edition, edited by Julie Ann Godson, also records a lost way of country life when cows were milked by hand, cheeses made on the farm, and the journey to market was by pony and trap. Includes masses of information for family history buffs.

1066: OXFORDSHIRE AND THE NORMAN CONQUEST
Why it all started and finished in our county

IT WAS AN EVENT which changed the country forever. And from the birth of a prince to the formal surrender after the Battle of Hastings, Oxfordshire frequently provided the background for the board-room take-over that was the Norman Conquest of England.

www.julieanngodson.com
Facebook: @julieanngodson

Printed in Poland
by Amazon Fulfillment
Poland Sp. z o.o., Wrocław